IN THE FIRING LINE

IN THE FIRING LINE

THE JIM LEIGHTON STORY

**Jim Leighton and
Ken Robertson**

MAINSTREAM
PUBLISHING

EDINBURGH AND LONDON

First published in Great Britain in 2000 by
MAINSTREAM PUBLISHING COMPANY (EDINBURGH) LTD
7 Albany Street
Edinburgh EH1 3UG

ISBN 1 84018 357 8

A catalogue record for this book is available from the British Library

Typeset in Cheltenham and Giovanni Book
Printed and bound by Butler and Tanner Ltd, Frome and London

Contents

Preface

Writing this book was not something I decided to do on the spur of the moment; I have wanted to tell my story, warts and all, for some time.

It was simply a matter of choosing the right moment and I opted to wait, albeit a little impatiently, until my playing career, which has spanned not far short of a quarter of a century, was heading for the finishing line.

My new role at Pittodrie means that I won't play for Aberdeen's top team. Unless, that is, an emergency occurs, or a chronic goalkeeping shortage hits the dressing-room of Pittodrie. So there are no loose ends in this autobiography. Ending my playing career has also freed me of any inhibitions I might have had about telling the plain, unvarnished truth concerning an innings during which there has been no shortage of pain as well as pleasure.

I'm grateful, of course, for all the honours and prizes which the game has bestowed on me. Holding the European Cup-Winners' Cup in my arms after helping Aberdeen take the honours in Gothenburg in 1983 is a memory that will stay with me for the rest of my life.

But I also look back in anger at some of the cards that I was dealt in both club and international football. I've been hurt and humiliated and will be forever scarred by the memory of the agony I suffered after being dropped by manager Alex Ferguson (now Sir Alex) from Manchester United's team for their FA Cup final replay with Crystal Palace at Wembley in 1990. That was the prelude to me being tossed, with no sign of sympathy, on the soccer scrapheap. I found that hard to bear.

It was a long, hard road back to the top, with another unhappy experience after I returned to Scotland to sign for Dundee in 1992. But I made it.

I recovered my zest for the game with Hibs and stepped back into the international spotlight. The circle was completed when I joined Aberdeen for the second time in 1997. I knew it would be my last stop as a player, and I will be happy to be staying on at Pittodrie as a goalkeeping coach. With 91 Scotland appearances behind me I must surely have some advice worth passing on to others. And in this book I will be giving advice to those up-and-coming young goalkeeping prospects.

In the meantime, there is no doubt in my mind that overcoming set-backs which could have ended my playing days much sooner has made me a stronger and, I hope, better person than I was when I was busy collecting medals during my first spell with Aberdeen. My hope is that other players, especially those who find their careers under threat and see no light at the end of the tunnel, will take some encouragement from my story. They may find, as I did, that if you want it badly enough, there is always the possibility of being able to confound your critics and bounce back.

My biggest regret is that my family had to suffer along with me during my dark days. While my wife, Linda, was a rock, I would have given anything to spare our daughter, Claire, and son, Greg, from the cruel taunts which were hurled at them when their father was branded a failure. It is to them and my father, Sam, who encouraged me every step of the way, from gawky schoolboy footballer to Scotland star, that this book is dedicated.

I also want to offer a word of encouragement to all those youngsters, many of whom write letters to me, who fear that having to wear glasses may prevent them from making a name for themselves in the professional game. Let me put their fears to rest by confessing that without contact lenses, which I've worn for the past 20 years, I wouldn't have had a career worth writing about. In fact, I wouldn't have had a career at all!

I'm sorry I did not realise my dream of making it to 100 caps, but I'll explain, in due course, why I felt I had to retire from international football when I did. I did not need any contact lenses to see when it was time to quit Scotland's squad.

Playing all over the world has been a marvellous experience, and I'll be telling you about the things that have happened to me in foreign parts. I'll also tell you about the managers I've served under, the players I've most admired and, of course, the highs and lows of my participation in World Cup campaigns.

I have tried to be as honest as possible in telling my side of the story regarding the controversies in which I've been involved because that has always been my style.

For the record, there are only four Scottish club grounds at which I have not played – Cowdenbeath, East Stirling, East Fife and Stranraer. I'd like to have completed the set, but you can't have everything in this game and I've had more than my share.

Jim Leighton
October 2000

ONE

In the Beginning

You'll never guess what flashed through my mind as I stood in the tunnel waiting to face Brazil in the opening match of the 1998 World Cup finals. How, I wondered, had a boy who started life in a humble prefab in Kilbarchan, Renfrewshire, managed to reach such giddy heights? It was no more than a passing thought which popped, uninvited, into my head before Brazil won that game 2–1. But it helped me to appreciate a special occasion – the biggest in my long Scotland career – even more. This, I told myself as I looked out at a sea of colour in the magnificent Stade de France and prepared to play against such famous names as Ronaldo, Rivaldo and Roberto Carlos, was a moment which had been beyond my wildest dreams.

Strange, isn't it, how life works out? Just how strange, you can judge for yourself when I tell you that, to this day, I still do not know who decided that I should become a goalkeeper.

When I started playing for my primary school it was as a centre-half. Yet, when my head teacher told me to report for a trial for a Paisley and District selection, he also informed me, without explanation, that I was to be in goal. Perhaps it was because I was big and daft – two of the essential requirements for standing between the posts – that someone thought I should be given the opportunity to show what I could do in a role which was completely new to me.

While that little mystery remains unsolved, I've no complaints about the way in which an unexpected opportunity (and one that I did not particularly fancy) has served me. As I look at the caps, which mark my 91 games for Scotland – plus three appearances at Under-21 level – I have good reason to thank my unknown mentor.

There are other aspects of my football background which are even more unusual. They stem from the fact that I am the product of what is known as a 'mixed marriage' – my mother, Mary, being a Catholic, and my father a Protestant. Attitudes which still prevail, especially in the west of Scotland, can make that a problem. Particularly so for a boy who grew up, like the rest of his pals, in Kilbarchan as a Rangers supporter – yet attended a Catholic primary school in Johnstone, my place of birth. Can you imagine the endless abuse I had to endure in the playground and on the service bus which carried me on the three-mile journey to and from my home? Remember that this was an era of unprecedented success for Celtic, during which they collected nine championship titles in a row and became the first British club to win the European Cup. Making matters worse for me was the fact that Rangers lost their chance of claiming a European trophy within days of Celtic's Lisbon triumph when they fell to Bayern Munich in the 1967 Cup-Winners' Cup final in Nuremberg.

I was a regular attender at Ibrox from my early days at school, having persuaded my father, a Morton fan, to forget his allegiance to the Greenock club and take me there. I can still rhyme off the names of the players in a line-up I revered – Ritchie, Shearer, Caldow, Greig, McKinnon, Baxter, Henderson, McMillan, Millar, Brand and Wilson. In my innocence, I could not understand why my mother refused to allow me to wear my Rangers hat and scarf when I attended chapel on Sunday mornings. Despite my protests, she was adamant.

It was years later, when I came to realise that many of the taunts hurled from the Ibrox crowd were aimed at my religion, that the penny dropped and I stopped supporting my favourite team. It was a sad day. Ironically, I was watched by a Rangers scout, who even had conversations with my father about my future, when I was playing for Glasgow United. He quickly lost interest, however, when one of his spotting missions led to him seeing me in action for St Cuthbert's Roman Catholic High School. When it dawned on me that I had more chance of captaining Real Madrid than playing for Rangers, the team I had supported, it was a disheartening experience. That is why I applaud the radical change of policy at Ibrox that achieved lift-off during the stewardship of Graeme Souness. Rangers chairman David Murray deserves enormous credit for playing a key role in changing the stance his club once took over signing non-Protestants because it takes bravery, as well as vision, to challenge old ways in a divided city like Glasgow, where the best way to steer clear of pub arguments is by claiming to be a Partick Thistle supporter.

The blinkered fans of both Rangers and Celtic still manage to create an atmosphere of hate and hostility at Old Firm games, but any sensible person would back the moves these clubs have made against religious bigotry. Although Souness is very much his own man, I remember him speaking to me in Mexico about the possible reaction to him signing a Catholic player for Rangers. He was sounding out some of his World Cup team-mates about the advisability of such a move. The feedback was not encouraging, so

Graeme then asked us what we thought about him taking a Jewish player to Ibrox. I can't remember the verdict on that one, but I had a quiet smile to myself when Israeli star Avi Cohen became a Souness signing. Graeme really set the cat among the pigeons when he signed a big-name Catholic player, Mo Johnston. The fact that Mo was also an ex-Celt caused many a fan to choke on his breakfast.

As I look back to my youth, I find it hard to believe that I once lost interest in playing football. It happened when one of my pals, Billy Thomson, took my place in Glasgow United's team. I was so disillusioned – perhaps it was more a case of being in the huff – that I stopped playing for over a year.

Happily, I eventually recovered my enthusiasm for the game and Billy, who also went on to become a Scotland goalkeeper, remains a good friend. We still joke about the early days of our rivalry. The Ibrox connection was again in evidence when former Rangers goalkeeper Erik Sorensen signed me for Ayrshire Junior club Dalry Thistle. Erik, a Danish international, also made it his business to lick my skinny, 17-year-old frame into shape – and he showed no mercy. He made a crusade out of improving my goalkeeping skills, giving up his time so that I would enjoy the benefits of his personal tuition. Enjoy is the wrong word, though, for I suffered torture at his hands and came to suspect that he had borrowed some of his ideas from the Spanish Inquisition. So fearsome were Erik's sessions that they left me limp. I was also frightened to tell him when I had a day off work in case he would organise an extra session for me. Be that as it may, there is no doubt I am indebted to this man. He set standards for me, as well as preparing me for the rigours of Junior football. His diligence and patience were commendable.

I needed that preparation when I played for Dalry in tough Ayrshire mining villages, where referees can visibly age in the space of a mere 90 minutes and young goalkeepers are obliged to learn their trade the hard way. I soon found out that opposing forwards who muttered dark threats about what was going to happen to me when the ball came my way were men of their word. They battered the life out of me and, when I got back on my feet, they were only too happy to repeat the process. It was a tough school, but I gained invaluable experience from games in which bruising, physical contact was the norm. I also learned not to flinch when one of my tormentors reached out to give me a friendly pat on the head after the final whistle!

Signing for Dalry coincided with me starting my first job as a civil servant. My place of work was the unemployment benefit office in Kinning Park, just along from Ibrox, and that, too, provided a sharp learning curve. I looked after the NFAs – people with no fixed abode – and what characters some of them were. My clientele included a doctor, dentist and a boxer. There was also a man with a wooden leg who crossed the Clyde on the Govan Ferry on his way to our office. He kept losing the leg on that journey – it once sailed down the river – and was full of amazing explanations for these mishaps. He never lost his sense of humour, or his willingness to give us a song. Like so many of these unfortunates who slept rough, life had not been kind to him. Yet I found he had a heart of gold.

It was in that office that I met Linda, the girl who would become my wife. She also worked in the same department and I was surprised to learn that she had attended the same primary school, though in a different year.

Our 'customers' took a great interest in our courtship, and I suspect we were toasted in some strange places, such as derelict buildings. My one-legged friend was sleeping in such a place when a demolition crew began knocking it down. He told the tale of a narrow escape with great gusto. There was also the strange case of a lady of the night who had her false teeth stolen, but I won't go into the details.

I had played a trial for Dumbarton, who did not fancy me, long before I signed a provisional form for Aberdeen in 1976. Celtic, who turned up on my doorstep a week later, were disappointed when they heard they were too late. There was, however, renewed speculation about my future when Morton supremo Hal Stewart was tipped off that the form I signed for Aberdeen had not been registered. Hal, a magnificent showman and ever the opportunist whose passing robbed the Scottish football scene of one of its most colourful characters, turned up at my Kinning Park office to see what was what. He also did his best to impress me by arriving in a huge *pink* car. It got him nowhere, but I have to admit I liked his style. Aberdeen chief scout Bobby Calder, another great character, was the man who made sure I was signed for Pittodrie. I was called up and farmed out to Highland League club Deveronvale the following year.

Although my mother would have preferred me to become a part-time player closer to home so that I could keep my civil service job, there was never any chance of me taking that route. There was nothing I wanted more than to have a crack at making the grade with a big club, and I liked both the people and the set-up at Pittodrie. I felt I would be given every chance to make my mark with Aberdeen and was, of course, proved right. Incidentally, when I was signed from my Junior club I received a £60 signing-on fee and a fiver a week. How times have changed! It has been my experience that you know very quickly whether you are going to enjoy being with a club. I had that feeling from the moment I first walked in the front door at Pittodrie, and it never wore off. That is why I count myself very lucky to be back there after spells with Manchester United, Dundee and Hibs.

My life would have taken a very different path if my father, a tricky left-winger in his day, had gone to England. Leeds United wanted to sign him, but when they turned up at the house it was only to discover that a much bigger outfit had beaten them to it. His call-up papers for the army had dropped through the letter box the previous day. Dad and I are best pals as well as father and son, but I can't even begin to imagine how disappointed he must have felt when he told Leeds that he could not join them. I'd like to think that in some small way I may have eased that disappointment for him by playing at the top level for so long. He doesn't drive, but he travels all over the country to watch me and I like to know he is sitting in the stand. I only have to look at his face after a game to know whether I have played well or not.

I'm much taller than him – six feet, one and a half inches to his five feet, eight inches – and that gave rise to an amusing tale after I had made a name for myself with Aberdeen. Asked what he had seen in the skinny youth he had signed from an Ayrshire Junior club, Bobby Calder replied that meeting my big, strapping father had allayed any fears about me filling out. Bobby, a legendary talent-spotter, could never resist embellishing his stories, but he certainly knew his business. He was responsible for a steady stream of good players landing at Pittodrie. Scouts like Bobby are worth their weight in gold, but I fear there are fewer seams for them to mine these days. It saddens me that the junior game, which pointed me in the right direction, no longer produces anything like the volume of talent that once abounded there.

TWO

Glory Days with Dons

I collected winners' medals galore – ten of them – during my first spell at Pittodrie, but could take no credit at all for Aberdeen's Premier Division championship title success in season 1979–80. I had made just one appearance in that League campaign, and it had been in a home defeat from Kilmarnock. In view of my non-contribution, I felt more than a little embarrassed about helping to show off the trophy and taking a bow in front of our support. I did not want to travel on the open-topped bus which was to carry Alex Ferguson's players on a tour through the city. The manager, however, insisted that I must join in and I'm glad I did. When I looked out over streets filled with our celebrating fans, I promised myself I would be back for more . . .

After the previous season, during which I had deputised for an injured Bobby Clark, I was back in the reserves. The only other first-team appearance I made in 1979–80 was in a Scottish Cup tie against Airdrie at Pittodrie. As we won that game 8–0, I had little chance to impress! Having said that, I saw no cause for complaint. My step back into the reserves was good for me in terms of my development as a goalkeeper. I'd also injured myself before the start of that championship-winning season – somehow managing, on a visit to Stornoway, to tear a cartilage while lying in bed! It was not until September that I was ready to undergo surgery, so I had plenty of spare time in which to analyse my shortcomings at top-team level. I left hospital determined to get my finger out and be much better prepared for my next chance of promotion. I did not have long to wait. Clark had a serious problem with his back just before the beginning of the 1980–81 season, and I replaced him from the start.

It was a great start. I got my hands on my first winners' medal straight away when Aberdeen beat St Mirren in the final of the Drybrough Cup at Hampden. It was typical of Clark, one of the nicest guys I have ever met, to send me a telegram conveying his best wishes before that game. We were unbeaten in our first fifteen League games that season, but we came a cropper in the European Champions' Cup after beating Austria Memphis in the first round. Our next opponents in that round, Liverpool, were far too good for us, winning 5–0 on aggregate. I had already played in Cup-Winners' Cup ties against Bulgarian club Marek Dimitrov and Fortuna Dusseldorf before I faced Austria Memphis, so I thought I knew a bit about the European scene when we took on Liverpool. I soon learned differently, however, for at that time the Anfield men were in a class of their own. They produced the only goal of the game at Pittodrie, Terry McDermott scoring after only five minutes. Then they handed us a 4–0 defeat on their own ground. All credit to Liverpool who had three Scotland stars – Alan Hansen, Graeme Souness and Kenny Dalglish – in their line up.

At Liverpool individual talents were dovetailed into a superbly organised team, and there were no apparent weaknesses for us to exploit. We were angry about Liverpool's early strike at Pittodrie because John McMaster, who had been detailed to mark

McDermott, was lying injured when that player scored. McMaster had been felled by a Ray Kennedy tackle which left a lot to be desired and later hastened the end of that fine player's career. I offer no excuses for us, however. Liverpool were far too accomplished to allow us space in which to play. The only good thing that came out of our two meetings with them were the lessons we learned, and I'll talk about that in the next chapter.

There was one amusing tale arising from our return game at Anfield, where it was customary for visiting goalkeepers to salute the Kop with a pre-match wave. I did so, having been given strict instructions about observing this ritual, and was given a fantastic reception. Ferguson must have missed that, for when we came in at half-time 2–0 down, he was raging at me.

'Why didn't you wave to them?' was his shouted question. 'But I did,' was my reply. 'Well, you didn't wave hard enough,' said Ferguson.

It was later, as we flew home, that Gordon Strachan had the last word – a cheeky one at that – on the subject. 'Look, Jim, there's a Liverpool fan down there,' he said, as he pointed out one of the plane's windows. 'You'd better wave to him!' Despite feeling down in the dumps, I couldn't help smiling. Strachan's crack topped Drew Jarvie's droll half-time comment at Anfield: 'Come on, lads, three quick goals and we are right back into this tie,' he told us. We finished runners-up to champions Celtic that season, but we all knew that Liverpool had set new standards for us.

Season 1981–82 brought me the first of my four Scottish Cup winners' medals. Our journey to Hampden started at Motherwell, where we won 1–0, and the remarkable thing about that goal was the speed at which it was scored. John Hewitt struck less than ten seconds after the kick-off. Hewitt was on the mark again when we beat Celtic 1–0 at Pittodrie and it could be said that he was the player who first pointed us in the direction of European glory the following season. We defeated Kilmarnock 4–2 in the quarter-finals and then met our manager's former club, St Mirren, in the semi-finals. A replay was required to dispose of our Paisley opponents. We drew 1–1 then won 3–2 at the second attempt.

Rangers got off to a good start in the Hampden final, when John MacDonald opened the scoring for them with a header in the fifteenth minute. It took us time to recover our composure after that setback, but Alex McLeish gave us the lift we needed when he produced a brilliant equaliser 12 minutes before half-time. Alex looked as if he was shaping up to make a pass, but then unleashed a great curling shot which flew inside the far post.

After that, both sides gave the impression that they were more concerned with avoiding defeat than lifting the trophy and the game slumped after the interval. It was a different story in extra time, however, for we then got the bit between our teeth and turned our superiority into goals. Mark McGhee beat Rangers goalkeeper Jim Stewart with a header from a Strachan cross only a couple of minutes into extra time and we went on to produce ample proof that we were not content just to defend our lead. Two more goals from Strachan (who was the game's star performer) and Neale Cooper gave us a resounding 4–1 victory.

Our after-match celebration was at the Gleneagles Hotel and we met film star Burt Lancaster. He was in Scotland for the making of *Local Hero* and, in view of the reception which awaited us in Aberdeen, that seemed quite appropriate. I needed no coaxing to board an open-topped bus on that occasion!

The first time you win something is always the best. I'll never forget how I felt during the last five minutes of that Scottish Cup final. I was so pumped up that I found it difficult to concentrate on the game and flew from my goal as soon as I heard the final whistle. I think Willie Miller was surprised to find me hugging him in the centre circle only seconds later because I'm not exactly fleet of foot. Perhaps I was wearing wings that day. It certainly felt like it.

We again finished second to Celtic in the championship race that season, despite taking seven points out of eight against Rangers. There was also disappointment for us in the UEFA Cup. We made a brilliant start to our campaign in that tournament, eliminating holders Ipswich in the first round. I think that made observers of the European game sit up and start taking notice of us. After drawing 1–1 at Portman Road, we put Bobby Robson's team to the sword at Pittodrie. Peter Weir was absolutely marvellous in that 3–1 victory, ripping Ipswich apart at the seams. We overcame Romanian club Arges Pitesti in the next round, but then came unstuck against a Hamburg team that featured the great Franz Beckenbauer. We lost 4–5 on aggregate, but learned more valuable lessons at the hands of the Germans. Although we did not appreciate it at the time, we were on our way to stepping out of the European classroom and claiming a prize. For it was in the following season, 1982–83, that we made club history by collecting the European Cup-Winners' Cup in Gothenburg, but I'll go into that triumph in detail in the next chapter.

Meanwhile, I'll concentrate on our successful defence of the Scottish Cup. We beat Hibs, Dundee, Partick Thistle and Celtic on our way to another Hampden showdown with Rangers, but we were a long way from our best in the final. As it came only ten days after our Gothenburg triumph in extra time, we were absolutely drained. There was very little left in the tank and I'm not surprised we appeared lethargic. It took an extra-time goal, scored by Eric Black in the 116th minute, to give us victory over Rangers, and by that time our legs had turned to jelly. Although our Hampden win completed an historic Cup-Winners' Cup and Scottish Cup double, my memories of that game are not happy ones. Although I thought I'd done well in the first 90 minutes against our Ibrox rivals,

Ferguson gave me a real tongue-lashing. 'You're Rangers' best player,' he snapped at me as we prepared ourselves for another helping of extra time.

Worse was to follow in the wake of our victory. When chairman, Dick Donald, brought the celebratory champagne into the dressing-room, Ferguson was in an even bigger rage. 'Keep the corks in that champagne,' he instructed. 'Willie Miller and Alex McLeish won that cup for us and I'll be looking for nine new players next season.' We were stunned. It seemed incredible that we were being lambasted by our boss at a time when we should have been savouring another success. What we did not know was that at the time Ferguson had also made his displeasure public by blasting us on radio and TV.

We went back to St Andrews that night, but some of the players were so disgusted with the manager's reaction to our victory that they stayed away from what was supposed to be a celebratory party. There was a dreadful feeling of anti-climax within our ranks. I've never since known anything quite like it. Ferguson knew he'd gone well over the top when he saw the newspaper headlines the next day and apologised to us. The damage was done, however, and we did not feel like forgiving him.

We took our revenge on Hamburg in season 1983–84 by beating them in the European Super Cup. Goals by Neil Simpson and Mark McGhee gave us our 2–0 win over them at Pittodrie after a 0–0 draw in Germany. On paper, at least, that made us the best team in Europe because Hamburg were, of course, the Champions' Cup holders. It was a nice feeling.

What we did prove that season, beyond any shadow of a doubt, was that we were Scotland's best. We won the Premier Division championship crown with what was then a record 57 points, and kept hold of the Scottish Cup. Combined with our Super Cup success, it added up to a fabulous treble. We were disappointed, of course, when we failed to retain the Cup-Winners' Cup. But with hindsight it was no disgrace to lose to Porto at the semi-final stage. They were an excellent team, fast emerging as a major force in Europe, and showed their class in home and away wins (both 1–0) over us. To be honest, our players thought they were in luck when we were paired with the Portuguese club because the other semi-final was between Manchester United and Juventus. Porto showed us the folly of making such assumptions before they themselves fell to Juventus in the final.

Back home we clinched the championship title at Tynecastle, where a Stewart McKimmie goal, his first for Aberdeen, gave us a 1–0 victory over Hearts. That gave me the medal I had longed for ever since that bus journey in 1980, four years earlier. More glory beckoned in the Scottish Cup, for we were back in another final, disposing of challenges from Kilmarnock, Clyde, Dundee United and Dundee on the way. Our ties with Kilmarnock and Dundee United had required replays, so we had six games behind us by the time we prepared to clear the last hurdle against Celtic at Hampden.

I can tell you now that I came within a whisker of missing that final.

In fact, the accident that I was involved in on the Monday prior to that game could have ended my career. I was at home, cutting the grass and looking after our two children, when my electric lawnmower became choked with grass. I was trying to free the blades with my hand when my daughter Claire, who was then only three, moved the switch on the handle. Oddly enough, I'd been looking at a warning about disconnecting the lawnmower before cleaning it only seconds earlier. I'd ignored it and paid the price. When Claire accidentally put the power back on, a flying blade sliced open the pinkie of my right hand and there was blood everywhere. It could have been worse. I might have lost fingers and ended my days as goalkeeper in that careless moment. But my injury was serious enough – especially with the final looming – and

I was in a panic. Leaving the children with a neighbour, I dashed to hospital. There, I found myself sitting next to a Celtic supporter. He made me feel worse when, after studying the blood-soaked towel wrapped around my hand, he announced that he intended to phone Celtic manager Billy McNeill and tell him I was injured. I could have killed him.

I made a point of arriving early at Pittodrie the next morning. I did not want my manager to hear the bad news from anyone else. I sat in his office along with Teddy Scott, Aberdeen's jack of all trades, to await him. I think Teddy was as nervous as I was when we heard Ferguson whistling as he walked through the corridor. 'I think I'd better prepare him for this,' he said before hurrying out of the room. When the whistling stopped I knew what to expect. At first the manager just looked at me as if he could not believe what he had just heard from Teddy. Then he called me all the silly buggers under the sun. I was told I should not have been cutting the grass *or* playing with my children in a cup-final week. When Ferguson's tirade subsided, he told me to go home and stay away from Pittodrie during the build-up to Hampden. With so many interviews and photo-calls going on at our ground, he was afraid that word of my injury would leak out.

He was entitled to feel apprehensive, for Aberdeen is like a village in terms of gossip. I had ample proof of that over the next few days when my team-mates phoned to tell me about the wild stories which were circulating about my mishap. Rumour had it that I had lost a finger, cut off my hand or electrocuted myself. But the best tale of all emanated from one of Gordon Strachan's neighbours. According to his information, I was dead. He also said I would not be playing at Hampden, which, in the circumstances, seemed pretty obvious!

Although I still had the stitches in my finger, I was able to help Aberdeen complete a memorable hat-trick of Scottish Cup final wins the following day when we beat Celtic 2–1. It was also the third time in a row that extra time had been required to settle the destination of this trophy. Eric Black put us in front, but Paul McStay equalised for Celtic – down to ten men after the first-half dismissal of Roy Aitken – four minutes from the end of normal time. Mark McGhee, who had been brought down by Aitken in the ordering-off incident, scored our winner in the 98th minute. Somehow or other, my accident had been kept quiet. But Celtic physio, Brian Scott, provided an interesting postscript to the affair when I met up with him on Scotland duty. He said that there had, indeed, been a phone call to Celtic Park from someone in Aberdeen who wanted to inform our rivals that I was injured and doubtful for the final. The tip-off had been dismissed as just another of the many crank calls which football clubs receive.

Our team broke up after those successful days, with three key players – Strachan, McGhee and Doug Rougvie, who had become a cult figure at Pittodrie – moving on. The new arrivals were striker Frank McDougall from St Mirren and full back Tommy McQueen from Clyde.

We had given ourselves a hard act to follow, but were delighted to continue our winning steak in 1984–85. In the circumstances, retaining the championship crown was a magnificent achievement We also did it in some style, winning 14 out of our 18 away games and setting a new record points total of 59.

McDougall was our leading marksman with 24 goals – 22 of them in the League – and I am convinced that had he joined us earlier in his career, he would have played for Scotland. I have no hesitation in saying that I've never played with a better finisher. Billy Stark, another signing from St Mirren, scored 20 goals for us that season – a marvellous contribution from a midfield player. The low points of that season were our early exits from two competitions – the Skol League Cup and the European Champions' Cup. We failed to progress beyond the first round in both of them. Airdrie were our Skol Cup conquerors, beating us 3–1 at Broomfield, while East German club Dynamo Berlin showed us the exit door from Europe.

We had beaten Dynamo 2–1 at Pittodrie, with Eric Black scoring both our goals. The East Germans won by the same score in Berlin and, after extra time, Dynamo won a penalty kick decider 5–4. We also lost our hold on the Scottish Cup after reaching the semi-final stage. Our first meeting with Dundee United at Tynecastle ended in a goal-less draw but United ended our unbeaten run in this tournament by winning the replay 2–1.

The League Cup was the only domestic trophy which had eluded us during our golden era. We put that right in season 1985–86. We also did it without conceding a goal. Over six ties, which included a replay with Dundee United, we never once allowed the opposition to score. Bryan Gunn, my understudy at Pittodrie, had two clean sheets, while I had four, including our 3–0 victory over Hibs in the Hampden final.

As Aberdeen had never won this competition under manager Ferguson, we were delighted to rectify that. Nor were Hibs allowed to stand in our way. Black opened the scoring after only nine minutes and Stark added another, three minutes later. Our Edinburgh rivals were heading for defeat before they knew what had hit them. Black completed the scoring with his second goal arriving in the 62nd minute. Former Hibs assistant manager Tommy Craig has since told me that our opponents lost that final before kick-off. It seems that some of their players were unnerved by the business-like looks they saw on the faces of the first three Aberdeen men – Miller, McLeish and myself – as we came out of the tunnel.

That season also saw us regain the Scottish Cup. We defeated Montrose, Arbroath, Dundee (after a replay) and Hibs on our way to a final against Hearts. Our game at Arbroath, where we won 1–0, sticks in my mind because Gayfield lived up to its reputation of being the windiest ground in Britain (probably the world).

The gale was so ferocious that we could not believe the tie was going ahead. It was farcical. When I tried to take a goal-kick against the wind, the ball was simply swept back into the arc of the 18-yard box for Alex McLeish or Willie Miller to head away. Not for the first time, I learned that local knowledge can be a valuable asset. When it was the Arbroath goalkeeper's turn to face the wind, he did not even try to send the ball upfield. All his goal-kicks were booted out of the pitch for throw-ins. A Joe Miller goal, scored just after half-time, gave us our 1-0 victory, and I was mighty glad to get off that pitch.

I had another Scottish Cup final injury scare that season. This time it was because of my attempts to keep fit while recovering from a broken finger, which had ruled me out of Scotland's game against Romania at Hampden. I thought it would be a good idea to play tennis, a sport in which my damaged left hand would not be involved. That turned out to be a *big* mistake. I tripped over a stone and tore my ankle ligaments. With the final just four weeks away, I feared the worst. To compound the matter, I could not tell my manager that I had hurt myself playing tennis of all things. A white lie seemed the best bet, so I informed him that the injury had occurred while I was playing with my kids. It was bad news when I saw a specialist ten days before the final. 'Forget it,' he told me, adding that if I managed to recover in time to play for Scotland in the World Cup finals in Mexico, I would be a very lucky man. I could not have felt worse after listening to that verdict on my ankle. There was, it seemed, not a glimmer of hope for me.

I was sitting at home, brooding over the specialist's words, when the phone rang. The call was from Neale Cooper and he wanted to tell me about Ian Law, a professional wrestler. It transpired that treatment from Law had helped Cooper to overcome a troublesome injury, and his suggestion was that I should see what he could do for me. 'Law says he'll get you fit,' said Neale. It seemed highly unlikely that a wrestler could cure my particular problem, but after giving Neale's tip some thought, I decided I had nothing to lose.

I was still dubious after receiving manipulative treatment from Law, but had a pleasant surprise when I went home and took off my shoe and sock. My ankle, which had been badly swollen, was now half its previous size. I saw Law again, with a great deal more enthusiasm, on the Saturday. This time his treatment brought about a dramatic improvement. So much so, that I felt ready to prove my fitness in a reserve match against Rangers at Ibrox on the Tuesday night. I passed that test with flying colours and, against all the odds, claimed my place in the final. Ferguson phoned my home on the night after my comeback in the reserves. Linda took the call and asked him if he wanted to speak to me. 'No,' said the manager, 'just tell him that if he goes near that bloody grass this week, I'm going to kill him.' This was a reference to my previous mishap with the lawnmower. Ferguson has a very retentive memory.

Hearts were still nursing disappointment over being pipped by Celtic for the championship when we met them at Hampden. It showed, too, for they were never really in the hunt after Hewitt gave us an early lead. We won 3–0, with Hewitt scoring again in the second half and Stark producing our third. Eric Black was dropped from that final – which gave me my fourth Scottish Cup winners' medal – after informing the manager that he was joining the French club Metz.

We reached the semi-final of the European Cup-Winners' Cup that season, and went out without losing a tie. Our semi-final rivals, Gothenburg, drew 2–2 with us at Pittodrie and, of course, the 0–0 draw in Sweden put them through by virtue of the away-goals rule. I missed the first leg, but was back for the return in the Ullevi Stadium – the scene of our 1983 triumph. Keeping a clean sheet was no consolation when we found ourselves out of the competition.

It was in November 1986 that we came to the end of Ferguson's highly successful reign with Aberdeen. He left Pittodrie that month to seek new challenges with Manchester United. His assistant, Archie Knox, looked after the team following his departure. But only briefly. He soon followed Ferguson to Old Trafford. Ian Porterfield was then appointed manager.

We had already made our exit from the European Cup-Winners' Cup before our change of manager. Sion, the Swiss club we had thrashed four years earlier, put us out in the first round. We'd beaten Sion 2–1 at Pittodrie, with our goals coming from Jim Bett and Paul Wright, but the Swiss left us smarting by scoring three times without reply on their own ground.

Celtic knocked us out of both the Skol League Cup and Scottish Cup, and I was sick of the sight of their international goalkeeper, Pat Bonner, by the end of that season. Including two matches against the Republic of Ireland, I faced him nine times. That must surely be some kind of record. And this statistic is even more remarkable because I missed one of Aberdeen's League matches against Celtic that term. It could have been ten. There were three meetings in the Scottish Cup, with Celtic winning the second replay, and another in the Skol League Cup. Another interesting fact is that six of the nine games produced draws. Although Celtic dismissed us from the Skol, it was on penalty kicks. The teams were locked on 1–1 after extra time. I felt like telling Pat we could not go on seeing each other so often or people would start talking about us.

I knew I would be leaving Aberdeen at the end of the season 1987–88 and was keen to add another medal to my collection before I packed my bags. I thought the Skol League Cup might provide it, for we reached the final. But there was no joy for us there. Our meeting with Rangers was one of the most exciting games I've ever played in, with the teams locked in a 3–3 draw after extra time, but Rangers then won the penalty shoot-out.

We finished fourth in the championship, just as we had done the previous season. It saddened me to end my 13-year association with Aberdeen, but I had reached the stage where I felt I had to leave. Like Ferguson, I wanted to test myself in new surroundings.

Little did I know then that I would one day return to Pittodrie.

THREE

Swedish Rhapsody

The Swedish city of Gothenburg will always have a special place in my heart. It was there, on a rain-soaked pitch at the Ullevi Stadium on 11 May, 1983, that I helped Aberdeen make history by winning the European Cup-Winners' Cup. It was their first European trophy. It was also the first time that a Scottish club other than the Glasgow giants, Rangers and Celtic, had collected silverware in a UEFA tournament.

The passing years have helped me appreciate the magnitude of Aberdeen's achievement. I find it a sobering thought that the odds are now hugely stacked against them repeating such a feat. For a start, the reorganisation of UEFA's competitions has led to the demise of the Cup-Winners' Cup. But that is only one of the changes which make it increasingly difficult for the Aberdeens of this world to earn European glory. The major factors are the wealth and resources of an elite group of clubs which now dominate that scene. They have proved that success can be bought and, as they grow richer, are distancing themselves from the rest. It's a bit like watching little rowing boats bobbing up and down in the wake of giant cruise ships . . . but not such a pretty sight.

Such thoughts were far from my mind as I set out on the road that led to Gothenburg. It was a very different era in which I made that journey, and I doubt whether anyone involved in football at that time could have foreseen how dramatically the face of our game would be changed. The idea of Scottish clubs recruiting talent on a world-wide basis then belonged in the realms of fantasy. Given the current situation, it seems strange to reflect on the fact that there were no foreigners (unless you count Darjeeling-born Neale Cooper!) in the Aberdeen team that triumphed in Sweden. In addition, most of us had grown-up and matured together. We were friends as well as team-mates and, by that time, had served an apprenticeship in Europe. Hard lessons had been learned from the likes of Liverpool, our conquerors in a previous Champions' Cup campaign, and we knew exactly what was required of us at this level. Because of this background, it was in a mood of confidence that we approached our first Cup-Winners' Cup test that season – a preliminary round tie against Swiss club Sion – and that confidence was not misplaced. We had a resounding 7–0 victory over the Swiss at Pittodrie – with our goals coming from Eric Black, Gordon Strachan, John Hewitt, Neil Simpson, Mark McGhee, Stuart Kennedy and Ballet (o.g.) – and that made the return leg a formality. We won 4–1 in Switzerland, with Hewitt, Willie Miller and two goals from McGhee. It was after his team's thrashing in Aberdeen that Sion's coach tipped us to go all the way and win the tournament. He was adamant that we would do so because we had strength in every department of our team. As it turned out, he was not a bad judge.

Our next opponents, Dinamo Tirana, reminded us that easy rides in Europe are few and far between. While far from being a quality side, the Albanians were responsible for giving us one of the most frustrating nights we had suffered in our own backyard. Dinamo simply set up camp in their own box and refused to budge. All we had to show for our relentless pressure was a Hewitt goal that gave us a 1–0 victory. It was a slender lead to take abroad, even though we could not see Dinamo confronting us with any new problems in Tirana. The concern was simply that this was very much a trip into the unknown where local conditions would be of paramount importance. The searing heat we encountered in the Albanian capital turned out to be the biggest of the 'X' factors, but our team showed great fortitude and character in battling their way to a 0–0 draw. The only thing we lost was a bit of weight!

Polish club Lech Poznan were the next visitors to Pittodrie and they contributed to a really good game. We won 2–0 through goals by McGhee and Peter Weir. That put our tails up for the return leg in Poznan and our control and composure was reflected in a 1–0 victory for us there. Our scorer, Dougie Bell, did not always figure in our domestic line-ups, but his style made him an outstanding contributor in Europe. He seemed to run on castors and such was his brilliance in midfield that foreign opponents found him extremely difficult to contain. Clearing the Polish hurdle put us into the quarter-finals which were not due to be played until March. It was a good feeling to have that stage of the competition tucked away as a future treat. It also gave us more time to savour the draw, and what a mouth-watering prospect that offered – Real Madrid, Inter Milan, Barcelona and Bayern Munich were all in the last eight.

We felt, and not without cause, that we got the toughest of these big guns when we were paired with Bayern. Apart from their own massive reputation in Europe and stars like Karl-Heinz Rummenigge and Paul Breitner, there was the fact that in the past we had not played well against German clubs. Fortuna Dusseldorf, Eintracht Frankfurt and Hamburg had all shown us Europe's exit door in recent years. All things considered, it was hardly surprising that the draw put an extra edge on our training sessions from then on. No Aberdeen player worth his salt wanted to be left out of a tie that had us, as well as our fans, in fever-pitch excitement. This was the real big-time stuff. The games you dream of playing in.

Our preparations for the first leg of the tie in Munich's magnificent Olympic Stadium could not have been more thorough. We studied videos, familiarised ourselves with Bayern's style of play and noted the strengths and weaknesses of their key players. We needed no extra motivation, although it must be said that the pre-match comments which came out of Bayern's camp helped to strengthen our resolve. Having noted the ages of our young players such as Black, Hewitt, Simpson and Cooper, we were labelled, somewhat dismissively, as a 'bunch of kids'. Much less complimentary was the judgement of a Bayern player who, after studying photographs of our players, branded us 'a bunch of thugs'. That comment was inspired by a marked lack of front teeth in photographs. I have to admit that Doug Rougvie, Stuart Kennedy, Dougie Bell and myself – we had lost around 20 front teeth between us – might have given the wrong impression! Anyway, we used that jibe to our advantage and made our gap-toothed grins look as fierce as possible in the tunnel before the first leg. I'll never know whether that made any impression on Bayern's players, but it did not seem to do us any harm. The so-called 'thugs' battled their way to a 0–0 draw and returned to Aberdeen with their heads held high.

We knew we were still a long way from victory because of our failure to score in Germany. Bayern had the kind of team that was well equipped to produce an away goal and we needed no reminding that a score draw in Aberdeen would put them through. Our worst fears were realised when Klaus Augenthaler rifled a 20-yard shot into my net after only ten minutes. It was only the second goal I had conceded in the competition, but that was no consolation. It gave us a mountain to climb because Bayern then proceeded to defend their lead with Teutonic thoroughness. It was not until seven minutes from the interval that we got the break we had been searching for from Neil Simpson. He went in like a tank to score from close range and put us back on level terms. We were in trouble again when Pfluger scored Bayern's goal in the 61st minute and I'm sure many of Aberdeen's fans thought we were on our way out of Europe following that set-back. After all, even another equaliser would not have been enough to save us from elimination because any kind of scoring draw would have put the Germans in the semi-finals. We were well and truly up against it and in desperate need of something special to rescue us.

It arrived in the 77th minute via a ruse that came straight from our training ground. Gordon Strachan and substitute John McMaster went into a well-rehearsed routine by seeming to get in each other's way in the taking of a free-kick. The pair then pretended to argue and, as a bemused Bayern defence temporarily lost their concentration, Strachan quickly took the kick from which Alex McLeish headed us back to equality. While that little piece of play-acting was not new to observers of the Scottish football scene, it certainly fooled Bayern. Nor were they given any time at all to dwell on being hit by a classic sucker punch. Pittodrie went wild when, only 60 seconds later, another Aberdeen substitute, John Hewitt, scored our third goal. It was the stuff of fairytales, for Hewitt's goal proved to be the winner. Somehow, we had found the will to come back from the dead and I'm sure the mighty roar from our fans at the end of the tie was tinged with just a little bit of disbelief.

I'm also sure that no one will remember that we did not play particularly well on that eventful evening. It was a clear case of the result and our dramatic comeback overshadowing all our shortcomings. Bayern general manager, Uli Honess, provided an interesting postscript to the tie when he said that , in defeat, he had been proved right. He said he had kept telling people that Aberdeen was a better team than Real, Barcelona or Inter but that no one had believed him. He also claimed that Aberdeen would go on to lift the trophy in Sweden because he could not see any of our rivals stopping us. Among the people who shared the Bayern chief's view was Aberdeen's official travel agent. He revealed that he had provisionally booked 1,600 beds in Gothenburg *before* the Dons had beaten the Germans to claim their place in the semi-finals. There's confidence for you.

Luck favoured us in the semi-final draw, for we got what we wanted – a pairing with Belgian club Waterschei. It strengthened the feeling that something special might be in store for Aberdeen at the end of the road, and that feeling spread through our squad. We did not, I hasten to add, underrate Waterschei. They had proved themselves strong enough to beat Paris St Germain in their quarter-final, but it seemed to us that the Belgians would be less formidable than the other semi-finalists – Real Madrid and Austria Vienna – and we were pleased to have them as our next opponents.

I think Waterschei were apprehensive about their first-leg visit to Pittodrie because of the circumstances in which we had overcome Bayern. They knew they would have a fight on their hands and that we would be difficult to discourage. At any rate, they were no match for us. We handed them a 5–1 beating, with Black, Simpson, Weir and McGhee (2) producing our goals. The only consolation for the Belgians was that they managed to escape total humiliation. It is no exaggeration to say that we might have doubled our winning margin on a night when we simply brushed aside our rivals. The trouble with such an emphatic win was that, in a strange way, it made us a bit nervous about the return leg. We knew our supporters would be travelling to Belgium with sky-high expectations, and our concern was that we might disappoint them by failing to produce another convincing win. While our lead looked impregnable, there was always the possibility of us losing our unbeaten record and we did not relish the prospect of that happening one little bit. Our fears were well founded, for Waterschei won 1–0. We were through to the final but there was a dreadful feeling of anti-climax in our dressing-room. It was like a morgue. We felt we had let ourselves down, as well as our fans. Our first defeat left a bitter taste in our mouths. The bottles of champagne that had been delivered to our dressing-room were left unopened. None of us felt like celebrating and that mood prevailed even after we had made the short trip back over the Dutch border to our hotel in Maastricht.

Another reason for our air of depression was the injury suffered by full-back Stuart Kennedy, who had twisted his knee on Waterschei's poor pitch. Even at that stage the injury looked serious enough to threaten Stuart's career, and we all felt sad about the prospect of losing the services of a fine Scotland defender whose pace and stamina had been so important to us at home and abroad. Stuart, a former marine engineer who was working in Grangemouth docks and playing part-time football for Falkirk when Ally MacLeod bought him for Aberdeen in 1977, never kicked another ball for us. We lost a father figure, as well as a key member of our team and one of the bravest players I've ever met. Even before that fateful moment in Belgium, everyone at the club knew that he had fought a constant battle and could not have continued playing as long as he did without taking pain-killing injections three times a day to combat a long-standing pelvic condition.

When it sank in that we had reached the final and would be meeting the mighty Real Madrid in Gothenburg, we could think of little else. It is fair to say that our Cup-Winners' Cup campaign had already affected our Premier Division championship bid, but the prospect of a showdown with the Spanish aces was even more distracting. It was, of course, a fantastic feeling to be contemplating a meeting with one of the most magical names in world football –

the club that had won the first five European Champions' Cup finals, including that marvellous 7–3 victory over Eintracht Frankfurt in front of a 135,000 crowd at Hampden. They had also enjoyed a sixth success in that tournament in 1966, the year before Celtic's Lisbon triumph. There was no doubting their pedigree.

Real's manager, Alfredo Di Stefano, was part of his club's legend and, without doubt, one of the finest and most complete players the world has ever seen. Capped by Spain as well as his native Argentina, he gained managerial experience in both countries – and Portugal – before returning to Real as their boss. We knew, right from the start of our preparations for the final, that the key to success would lie in how we handled Real's intimidating aura. They had a famous name and a famous all-white strip, but as manager Alex Ferguson was quick to point out, neither of these things made them invincible. We also reasoned that in terms of team spirit we had a definite edge. We had a family feeling in our squad that at times made us believe that we could beat anyone. Gothenburg was one of those times, for not one of Aberdeen's players travelled to Sweden entertaining the thought that we might lose.

It may well be true that the rain in Spain falls mainly on the plain, but in Gothenburg it seemed to concentrate all its efforts on landing on the Ullevi Stadium. If it wasn't for the tarpaulins that covered the playing surface before the match, I doubt whether the final could have gone ahead as scheduled.

We got off to a marvellous start when Eric Black, still a teenager, opened the scoring in the seventh minute. But that heavy, sodden pitch was responsible for us conceding an equaliser only eight minutes later. In normal conditions an Alex McLeish pass-back would have reached its destination without any problem, but it stuck in the mud and I brought down Santillana as he rushed in to profit from the situation. Italian referee Gianfranco Menagali had no hesitation in awarding Real a penalty and it was the correct decision. I could only curse the weather as Juanito stepped forward to beat me from the spot. Thunder rolled and lightning flashed, but there were no more scoring fireworks for the rest of the 90 minutes. Despite that, Aberdeen had taken a firm grip of the game in the second half, and we went into extra time looking a fitter and more positive side than a visibly tiring Real. Our reward came in the 112th minute when substitute John Hewitt, who had replaced Black, beat Real goalkeeper, Augustin, with a header. The super sub (how John hated that title) had struck again, just as he had done against Bayern, and we knew victory was in our grasp.

Although we were well on top, there was a moment of danger for us just before the final whistle when Real were awarded a free-kick on the edge of the box. It was a tense moment and, as he stood in our defensive wall, Peter Weir decided to take out insurance. 'Please, God, don't let them score,' he implored. Peter's prayer was answered, and there was bedlam in the stadium after that as 10,000 rain-soaked Aberdeen fans who had travelled to Sweden by land, sea and air, saluted our success.

We relished that salute because there had been nothing fortuitous about our victory. We deserved it. I had been obliged to make only one good save during the final, while Real's Augustin had made some unbelievable stops to keep us at bay. He had also enjoyed some timely rescues by his defenders. It was good to see crocked Stuart Kennedy – given a place on the subs' bench for that very reason – collecting his medal. But I felt really sorry for Dougie Bell whose injury had kept him out of the final and a showpiece game he would have relished. As I now know, the disappointment of missing out on one of football's big occasions is not something that can be easily wiped from a player's memory. It is in the nature of things – important games seem to be all over in a flash – that I did not realise how well Aberdeen had played until I watched a video of the final. I must confess, however, that the aftermath of that game is even more difficult to recall. I do remember watching Aberdeen fans, who probably reasoned that they could not get any wetter, cavorting in the fountain outside the stadium as we left to return to our hotel outside the city.

Our wives were waiting for us there, and an all-night party ensued. This time the were no refusals when the champagne corks popped. Everyone got into the swing of things and a few players decided to get wet all over again by jumping into the hotel pool fully clothed.

We were given an amazing homecoming when we returned to Aberdeen. Every street our open-topped bus passed through on the journey from the airport to Pittodrie was lined with cheering people. Whole families came out of their houses to greet us and I don't think I've ever seen so many smiling faces. Who said Aberdeen folk were loath to let their hair down and have a party?

I think we were still running on adrenalin (and possibly alcohol) when we hammed Hibs 5–0 in front of a full house at Pittodrie only three days after our strength-sapping extra-time victory in Gothenburg. We finished third in the League, only a point behind table-topping Dundee United, the other half of Scottish football's New Firm, and still had a Scottish Cup final against Rangers to look forward to the following Saturday. Life was good. And it was even better when we cleared that hurdle. I believe that only Celtic's immortal Lisbon Lions could be compared with the Aberdeen team of that time.

While the current Rangers team is certainly the strongest I've seen in my lifetime – and remember that I watched them as a boy – I do not rate them as highly as my Gothenburg pals. We had power and stamina, as well as skill. We also had the kind of resilience that is needed to win games against Rangers and Celtic in Glasgow. Foreign strongholds held no fear for us either, and we proved that on a number of occasions. It saddened me when, in their wisdom,

UEFA bosses decided to scrap the Cup-Winners' Cup because it made no small contribution to the European scene and gave a lot of smaller clubs the chance to make a name for themselves.

I'll miss it.

By the way, I'm sure that Real Madrid's success in Paris, where they were crowned kings of Europe for the eighth time, must have taken quite a few Aberdeen supporters on a trip down memory lane. It may also make some people look back at what our team did in Gothenburg with increased respect.

FOUR

I Join United

My transfer to Manchester United in May, 1988, was not as straightforward as it may have seemed at the time. There were protracted, behind-the-scenes negotiations between manager Alex Ferguson and myself before the deed was done. There was also a clandestine meeting in circumstances that would have earned the approval of James Bond, but more of that later. Put simply, the situation was that, in addition to getting a bargain buy from Aberdeen, Ferguson wanted, quite rightly, to hire my services as cheaply as possible. As far as my personal terms were concerned, he held the advantage of knowing exactly what I was earning at Pittodrie. What he did not know, however, was that thanks to two Scotland team-mates who were on United's staff – Gordon Strachan and Brian McClair – I was well informed about the wage structure at Old Trafford.

It was checkmate!

Ferguson made regular calls to my home in Aberdeen after he became United's boss. He knew I fancied a move. He also knew that Aberdeen could lose a sizeable slice of any transfer fee they might get for me if, on the completion of my contract with them, I joined a foreign club. Under the transfer formula that was then in operation, I would have cost no more than £250,000. That situation helped Ferguson put pressure on Aberdeen to sell me to him. In fact, there was foreign interest in my future. There were approaches from two clubs, one German the other French, and I was offered the moon. More specifically, the French club promised me tax-free wages plus a free house and car.

There is no doubt that I would have been sorely tempted to pack my bags and move my family abroad had that offer been put in writing. The truth is, however, that I found the prospect of joining United irresistible. I also knew that if I turned down the opportunity to play for one of the world's most famous clubs, it would never again come my way.

It would be fair to say that my secret telephone conversations with Ferguson did not always run smoothly. My estimation of my worth to United caused him to slam down the receiver on at least a couple of occasions. The negotiations continued, however, and sufficient progress had been made by the early part of 1988 for Ferguson to call me to a get-together with chairman Martin Edwards and himself in the west of Scotland around the end of February. It was, of course, a cloak and dagger meeting. Ferguson and Edwards couldn't afford to be seen talking to me or they would have been in serious trouble with the footballing authorities. That being the case, I had to borrow a friend's car for the drive down from Aberdeen. My own was unsuitable for a secret mission, as it displayed my name. As instructed, I met up with the United pair near Cumbernauld, just off the motorway. We then drove to a car park, where I left my vehicle and joined Edwards in his. The plan was for us to follow the manager's car to the home of one of his relatives. He was to indicate the house at which we were to stop and where the back door would be left open for us. Ferguson would drive past the house but return later. Car telephones ensured that the manoeuvre was completed without a hitch, but the same could not be said of the half-hour conference held in that house. I liked the sound of the plans outlined for me by Ferguson and Edwards, but there was still some haggling over wages.

Aberdeen tried to keep me, but the new terms offered by my manager Ian Porterfield – Ferguson's successor at Pittodrie – came nowhere near what I knew I could earn elsewhere. The club knew I was determined to better myself and, when they realised there was no way I could be persuaded to stay, became resigned to my departure.

Aberdeen's last game of the 1987–88 season – a no-score draw with Motherwell at Pittodrie – helped me establish a new club record of 35 clean sheets from 59 first-team matches. It was also my farewell appearance and I waved goodbye to the crowd as I left the pitch. At that point there was no official confirmation of where I would be playing the following season, but the fans already knew that it would not be in front of them.

When Ferguson phoned me on the Monday, he gave me the news I was waiting to hear. A deal had been struck with Aberdeen – £750,000 was the reported transfer fee but I was told it was less – and I was heading for England. Ferguson advised me to act surprised when Porterfield told me the deal was done. Strachan, who had done so much to keep me in the picture throughout my negotiations with United, was also on the phone.

Things moved very quickly after that. Linda and I were whisked down to Manchester so that we could look at houses. I was also given a medical that lasted almost a whole day. It started at 10 a.m., continued after a break for lunch, and finish at 4 p.m. I don't think that any part of my anatomy escaped scrutiny, and I had to laugh when I was asked if I could put my bandy legs together. 'Believe it or not, they are together,' I replied. The radiologist said it was the first time he had been obliged to take two independent shots of one pair of legs! By the way, the medical I was given by Dundee – the club I joined after leaving United – provides an interesting comparison. It consisted of a few questions and lasted less than two minutes. United, of course, do everything in the grand manner.

My jaw must have dropped when I was shown round Old Trafford, for I was overawed by my surroundings. I'd played there before, but hadn't appreciated the extent of the club's facilities.

I know the stadium is now even more magnificent than it was when I first stepped inside the front door as a United player, but at the time I would not have thought that possible. I signed for United six days after my farewell appearance at Pittodrie, and the date – Friday, 13 May 1988 – will be forever imprinted on my mind. I recall having a laugh with Martin Edwards when he asked me if I was superstitious. I'm not, but was later given cause to wonder about such things. I did not take the decision to join United without a great deal of thought. It was a huge step because it involved uprooting my entire family. Linda and I also knew that it would structure the rest of our lives. I knew United were a big club, and it did not take me long to discover that they were even bigger than I had previously thought. They enjoy a global support, and fans travel to their ground from all over Britain. On match days I found myself driving to Old Trafford behind coaches from Belfast and Glasgow, as well as all over England, and the scenes in the car park were like nothing I'd experienced in Scotland. So many autograph-hunters waited there that it could take you half an hour to gain entry to the stadium. Our players were treated like royalty, especially when we travelled abroad. I recall a remarkable trip to Bangkok where we discovered that Thai hotel waiters did, in fact, regard us as some kind of monarchy. They could not do enough for us.

There was little chance of instant glory for me in my first season with United because I joined what was then an average side. Our League campaign – I played in all of the 38 games – saw us finish in 11th place, and Nottingham Forest knocked us out of the FA Cup in the sixth round. It took us three games to overcome Queen's Park Rangers in the third round of the FA Cup and two to remove Bournemouth from our path in the fifth, so I had an eventful introduction to that competition. We had a good defensive record in the League until some of our players began putting on their holiday hats towards the end of the season. I learned a lot from my first season – some of it the hard way – and I'll never forget my first game against Wimbledon at Plough Lane.

I knew Wimbledon were a tough outfit – particularly on their own patch – but I didn't know how tough. It wasn't until I changed ends at the start of the match – pausing for a brief word with goalkeeper Hans Segers, that I realised I was about to find out. As I turned away from Segers, I was confronted by a pack of Wimbledon players, including Vinnie Jones, Lawrie Sanchez and John Fashanu. Much to my surprise, the group made it clear they were interested in my state of health.

'How's your back, son?' asked Vinnie with the kind of menacing smile that was later to earn him a film role as a villain. 'Fine,' I replied somewhat naïvely. 'Don't worry,' said Vinny reassuringly, 'we'll fix it for you.' I should explain that a back injury had prevented me from playing for Scotland in their World Cup qualifying tie against Yugoslavia at Hampden three days earlier. In fact, it was not until the Saturday morning that I passed a fitness test for the Wimbledon game. Vinnie's words were, of course, a clear warning that he and his mates intended to carry out their own tests.

I did not have long to wait for the first one, for it came with Wimbledon's first corner. Sanchez welcomed me to Plough Lane with a forearm smash which flattened me and knocked out a tooth. I lost two teeth and had my nose broken in my first three months with United, but that was by no means the only damage I suffered. I had so many stitches that I lost count.

Many of my injuries stemmed from goalmouth clashes with opponents who towered over me. I thought that at 6ft 1½ in. I was pretty tall, but that was obviously not the case in England's Division One. Giants seemed to abound there. Having said that, I enjoyed my change of scene and the opportunity to play in front of much bigger home crowds than I'd seen at Pittodrie. My first League game at Old Trafford – against Queen's Park Rangers – drew a crowd of 46,377, and I marked the occasion by keeping a clean sheet. As I had spent all my days in Scotland, everything was new and exciting and I was determined to win over the fans who occupied the Stretford End of our ground. I had been well warned that they were notoriously hard on goalkeepers, but I saw that as another challenge. I knew that if I could win them over, I would be well on my way to establishing myself as an Old Trafford favourite. It proved a hard nut to crack. Despite the fact that I got off to a really good start, I never felt they were with me. That was not for lack of trying on my part. Indeed, I tried so hard that I eventually made myself unwell, but I'll say more about that in the next chapter.

United's nation-wide appeal caused problems at our away games. It seemed that no matter where we went you could bet on there being a delayed kick-off. While we were jealous of Liverpool's success, they envied us our massive support. Despite what happened later, I found playing for United a fabulous experience and something I would not have wanted to miss. Nor did I have the problem of an unsettled wife. Linda enjoyed living in Cheshire and so did our kids. When the time came for us to leave our home in Wilmslow, they were in tears.

FIVE

My Old Trafford Nightmare

The Leighton family home in Aberdeen is full of souvenirs of my long career in football. What you will not find there, however, is even a solitary trace of my days with Manchester United. I've made a point of removing all trace of that period of my life because recalling what happened to me at Old Trafford still hurts. Even now I have to steel myself to talk about the nightmare into which manager Alex Ferguson, someone I once regarded as a friend, thrust me. So strongly do I feel about the way in which he handed me the cruellest blow of my life that there is not a hope in hell of that friendship ever being revived. Indeed, I have promised myself that I will never again speak to him. I don't see why I should, for it was his decision to drop me from United's FA Cup final replay with Crystal Palace in 1990 that led to me being cast, very publicly, into a soccer wilderness.

Ferguson's decision shattered me. To all intents and purposes it signalled the end of my career with his club. I knew that, just as surely as he must have done, from the moment he broke the bad news to me, and I cannot find it in my heart to forgive him. What also soured me was his lack of support both before and after that event. He distanced himself from me when I was trying to pick up the broken pieces of my life and never offered any encouragement. In fact, the only time we talked during the rest of my stay at Old Trafford – a year and nine months of absolute purgatory – was when I was summoned to his office, where we had several arguments. I felt like an outcast.

I have not allowed any of this to cloud my appreciation of Ferguson's achievements as a manager. How could I? The statistics of this soccer knight's success speak for themselves, and he has already claimed legendary status. I know, having played under him for Aberdeen and Scotland, as well as United, how relentless his pursuit of glory is. I also know, to my cost, that he has more than his fair share of the ruthless streak which is to be found in the make-up of all top managers.

By the time a reported £750,000 transfer fee enabled me to follow Ferguson from Aberdeen to United in the summer of 1988, I had already tasted the fruits of his leadership on several occasions. I was confident that he could help me win more prizes in England and gave no thought to the possibility of disappointment. I was, after all, an established international player who had already proved himself to the man at United's helm, so saw no need to feel apprehensive about the challenge which awaited me in new surroundings. I was ready to face that challenge. Perhaps it is just as well that we do not know what life has in store for us. If I had been blessed with second sight, I would never have left Pittodrie for Old Trafford.

Very little went wrong for me during my first spell with Aberdeen, and it is probably true to say that I had been spoiled by success. I don't think there is any doubt that, because of this, I was ill-prepared for what happened to me after United's first Wembley meeting with Palace which ended, after extra time, in a 3–3 draw.

With me being blamed for the loss of two goals, I was desperate to redeem myself and I thought I'd earned that chance, for I'd been an ever-present in United's cup campaign and had missed very few League matches. It was not to be, however.

I'll admit that I was not always in my best form that season. United got off to a sticky start and our supporters were unhappy with us. Never more so than when our local rivals, Manchester City, handed us a 5–1 thrashing at Maine Road in September. I think that heavy defeat marked a turning point. There was a sharp escalation in the flak I was taking from our fans after that. I became a prime target for the vociferous Stretford End and, among other things, was advised to 'F-off' back to Scotland. That kind of pressure was new to me and I did not handle it as well as I might have done. It seemed that the harder I tried to please, the more criticism came my way. I literally worried myself sick, developing a stomach ulcer and being plagued by bouts of migraine. I could have done with a public show of support from the manager, but it was not forthcoming. Perhaps he felt he had enough on his plate, for he, too, was under considerable pressure.

Some of his biggest critics were United players. In fact, he had lost the dressing-room, but I always stood up for him. Apart from chairman Martin Edwards, I was probably his staunchest supporter. What a pity he did not return the compliment when I most needed it.

Our FA Cup campaign got under way at Nottingham Forest's City Ground and we were not fancied to clear that hurdle. Forest were going well while we were struggling. We also kept hearing that our manager was only one game away from the sack, which did not help matters. Despite that scenario, a Mark Robbins goal gave us a 1–0 victory. The next stop was Hereford and again we scored, through Clayton Blackmore, the only goal of the game. The tie was played on a pitch like a ploughed field and in terrible weather. I felt we were very fortunate to leave that stage as winners. Our fifth-round tie, at Newcastle, was a cracker, generating the best atmosphere I played in during my stay in England. It was a see-saw game from which we did well to extract a 3–2 victory. A Brian McClair goal saw us conquer sixth-round opponents Sheffield United 1–0 in yet another away test and that earned us a tie much nearer home. Our semi-final, against Oldham, was at Manchester City's Maine Road. We drew 3–3 after extra time, but won the replay 2–1. It was next stop Wembley. After our drawn final there was talk of our manager's head being on the block if we failed to overcome Palace at the second attempt. What I did not know, of course, was that he was planning to bring down the axe on mine before the replay.

It happened on the eve of that game. Ferguson took me aside to tell me that I was out of his Wembley line-up and that Les Sealey would be taking my place. I've no clear recollection of what else was said because I was numbed by his decision. I could not see straight and was rendered speechless. I was also dreading the thought that my first task would be to call Linda to tell her my bad news. I knew it would devastate her and, when I plucked up enough courage to lift the phone, had my fears confirmed. Both of us were in tears during that conversation.

Sealey, who had joined United on loan from Luton Town, came to my room that night. Basically, he wanted to convey some sort of apology for taking my place. He also asked if I would do him a favour, but I knew what was coming, so I cut him short. 'No,' I told him, 'I don't want your medal.' When I then asked him if, in the same circumstances, he would accept a medal from me, I got the answer I expected. He shook his head. Despite my refusal, Sealey's gesture was appreciated. There is, as you may know, a feeling of brotherhood among goalkeepers. Getting through the next day proved to be one of the toughest tasks of my life. I was in a trance, hardly aware of all that was happening around me. But I knew I was not dreaming when I stepped out of the Wembley tunnel.

The first thing I saw was Sealey's name and number flashing up on the electronic scoreboard. As the decision to drop me had been kept a closely guarded secret that message provoked a noisy reaction from the crowd. United's fans howled at me as I walked round the track to take my place in the stand. I wished I could have made myself invisible, for every pair of eyes in the ground – 80,000 of them – seemed to be trained on me. It was a long, long journey to my seat. The match itself is a blur. I rarely have any difficulty in recalling details from matches I've watched, but not that one. I can tell you that a Lee Martin goal gave United their 1–0 victory, but that is about all. I'll give Sealey full marks for persistence, for he handed me his medal as I stood in the dressing-room after the game. I did not want to cause a scene, so I waited for the opportunity to slip it into the pocket of his jacket, which was hanging up. Linda had not wanted to attend the replay after my phone call, but I persuaded her to change her mind. My motive was a purely selfish one. I wanted her support at the match and on the train journey back to Manchester. I was glad of her company. Ferguson made a point of giving all the players' wives a celebratory kiss at Wembley Station, but Linda turned her back on him. She firmly denies, however, Ferguson's claim that she gave him two fingers.

When we returned to our home in Wilmslow, Cheshire, it was to find ourselves under siege. My shock removal from United's team had sparked a media feeding frenzy. Photographers were everywhere, even hiding in our bushes, as they tried to snatch pictures of me, and we became prisoners in our own home. So bad was the scene that I had to call on the local police to clear our garden and keep intruders at bay. It was hard enough coping with this sort of thing over one weekend, so how United and England star David Beckham is able to handle the constant harassment inflicted on him is beyond me. I couldn't live with that. Of course, with Scotland's opening match in the World Cup finals in Italy less than a month ahead, I had more to worry about than my severely damaged reputation as a United player. What concerned me, as you can well imagine, was that national team boss Andy Roxburgh might be wondering whether I was in a fit state of mind to face Costa Rica, Sweden and Brazil in our group ties. Thankfully, that was not a problem. Loyalty to the players who had served him well was one of Roxburgh's trademarks during his reign as Scotland's boss, and he backed me to the hilt. His public declaration that he was standing by me as his No. 1 World Cup goalkeeper was a much-needed tonic, and that is something I certainly won't forget.

Apart from a League Cup tie at Halifax the following season, I never made another appearance in United's first team. Nor were there more than a handful of outings at reserve level. I found training from Monday to Friday without the prospect of playing a game a soul-destroying experience. Loan spells with Arsenal and Reading helped break the monotony at Old Trafford, and I was extremely well treated at Highbury. Manager George Graham, who took me there as cover for England's David Seaman, steered Arsenal to the championship title that season, and insisted on involving me in every celebration. Goalkeeping coach Bob Wilson also made me feel at home and went out of his way to make sure he could work with me as often as possible. Ironically, one of my few conversations with Ferguson stemmed from the delivery of a package from the FA. It arrived three months after my Wembley heartbreak and contained the medal I had earned from playing in the first game against Palace. Secretary Ken Merrett shook my hand as he gave it to me, but I told him I did not want the medal and that it should be sent straight back from where it came. Ferguson was furious when he heard about my reaction and called me to his office. We had a row, with the manager claiming that I would live to regret my decision, but I never will. It is not something, as he suggested, that I would one day take any pride in showing my grandchildren.

What I've kept quiet, until now, is that had I helped United beat Palace in the first game, I would have asked for a transfer. I was not happy at Old Trafford and felt I could find more job satisfaction elsewhere. I scrapped that plan after what happened in London because I did not want people to think I was running away from Old Trafford with my tail between my legs. That is not, and never has been, my style. I'll always wonder why it was not until after he wielded his Wembley axe that Ferguson began saying nice things about me for public consumption. Not so nice is his assertion that I acted selfishly by refusing to accept any of the blame for being dropped. I'll counter that by telling you I could have made a fortune out of selling my side of the story in the wake of his decision. I chose, instead, to turn down every offer – including one that was the equivalent of a year's earnings. That doesn't sound very selfish to me.

I did consent to a newspaper article being written about me a week after the replay, and cash was not the motivating factor. For my family's sake, I simply wanted to put an end to some outrageous speculation about the reason for me being dropped. I was supposed to have been involved in a fight with another United player – Paul Ince was one of the names mentioned – or clashed with assistant manager Archie Knox. All of it was pure fiction. I also wanted to set the record straight about my reason for refusing the medal offered me by Les Sealey. When Ferguson got wind, as managers invariably do, of the impending publication of the article, he phoned me at home. Clearly, he thought I was going to slag him, but what he actually said was that chairman Martin Edwards was very much against me doing the piece. I listened to what he had to say, but after that conversation my immediate reaction was to phone the chairman. I wanted to hear his views on the subject for myself. Imagine my surprise, then, when an affable Edwards told me: 'Go and make yourself a few bob, son, but don't embarrass the club or yourself.' I made a point of having the article faxed to the chairman before its publication. He was the last person I wanted to let down.

Ferguson has since claimed he was so concerned about my well-being after I was criticised for losing a goal to Brazil in the World Cup finals that he tried to contact me at Scotland's camp in Italy. Well, the only call I remember getting from him in Italy was about tickets for each of our three group ties in Genoa and Turin. His own allocation had not turned up and he was looking for some assistance. It would have been easy for me to snub him and claim I could not help out, but I'm not the petty type. Tickets were available through the SFA, so I made sure his problem was solved.

SIX

Out of the Frying Pan

It was a cold day in February, 1992, when I flew home to Scotland to sign for Dundee, but it looked fine to me. I thought that the £200,000 deal struck with Manchester United had marked the end of my darkest days in football. There was, I'll admit, a niggling doubt in the back of my mind. Despite Dundee manager Iain Munro's assurances that the Dens Park club's ambitions matched my own, I had a premonition that this might not prove to be the case. I had been told that if I joined Dundee, my arrival would be the catalyst for other big-name signings, but I could not help wondering how a spending spree would be financed. There were no indications that the Dark Blues had unearthed a goldmine. I had no reservations about Munro's sincerity and it was because of his coaxing over a period of weeks that I finally agreed to the move. The feeling of being wanted, something I had not experienced for a very long time, was another factor that swayed me.

I flew north with my agent, Jerome Anderson, who found a telephone call awaiting him at Edinburgh Airport. It was from German club Werder Bremen and, much to my surprise, it transpired that they were keen to sign me. Their goalkeeper had been injured playing in a European tie the previous evening and they wanted me as an instant replacement. Finding myself in demand outside British football was a real tonic, but that was as far as it went. While the idea of playing at the top level in Germany was very appealing, I had to reject Bremen's proposition. I explained that I had promised to sign for Dundee and had no intention of breaking my word. Bremen went on to win the European Cup-Winners' Cup that season, beating Monaco in the final, and that made me feel like kicking myself for being so virtuous. But you can't change the way you are made. Earlier in this book I made the point that I usually knew, very quickly, whether I was going to enjoy playing for a club. Such was the case when I walked into Dens Park to complete my signing. Although I did my best to ignore them, the vibrations were not encouraging.

My instincts proved correct, for assistant manager John Blackley was sacked only days after my arrival and Munro's dismissal followed shortly afterwards. What a start. The changes earned rapid promotion for a much-travelled Englishman, Simon Stainrod, who was first given Blackley's job and then stepped up the ladder again to become player-manager. I did not like Stainrod – a cocky, arrogant type as a player – and found him even less endearing as a boss. My misgivings grew following his elevation, but I did not allow this to become a distraction. I wanted to savour again the taste of success and concentrated all my thoughts on helping Dundee make a return to the top flight in style, as First Division champions. This was duly achieved, but having arrived on the scene with only 13 League games left to play, I don't think I made much of a contribution. I'm sure Dundee would have been able to complete their task without me, although I had no complaints about adding another medal to my collection. Unlike the one sent to me in England, I was pleased to accept it.

As I had suspected, the players who followed me to Dens Park were modest rather than expensive signings. In fact, I still don't know why Dundee bought me. They clearly couldn't afford the cost of my transfer and signing-on fee – despite the fact that some of the monies due were to be paid in instalments – and the same applied to my wages. I was not impressed by the conduct of some of their players, either. In fact, if there had been a World Cup for drinkers, I can think of a few who would have qualified for selection. Having played with top professionals throughout most of my career, I was dismayed by their attitude and lack of self-discipline.

With my house in England still unsold – it had been on the market for two years – the first part of my time at Dundee involved me in a great deal of commuting. I was glad when that ended and I was able to move the family up to rented accommodation in a pleasant spot in Auchterarder, Perthshire, but my feeling of apprehension about what lay ahead of me on the football front persisted. I had very little in common with Stainrod and had sensed, from the moment he took over as manager, that he would look for an excuse to unload me. Whether that was simply a case of personal dislike, I do not know. Dundee probably felt they would have to get rid of me, for they owed me a sum in excess of £10,000. That, coupled with my wages and appearance money, added up to a powerful argument for dispensing with my services.

'How long do you think it will be before they bomb you out?' asked the voice of wifely intuition.

I did not have to wait very long for the answer to that question. It came in the early part of the following season when Stainrod dropped me after a 6–3 defeat from Partick Thistle at Firhill in September, claiming that I could not handle the new pass-back rule. I was devastated because I knew that verdict would be extremely damaging to my reputation. He might just as well have told the world I was crap, for that was the inference in his criticism of me.

As a matter of fact, Stainrod went out of his way to make sure that everyone in Scottish football knew his reason for demoting me. At that time, every goalkeeper was adjusting to the new rule – some more quickly than others – but I felt that Stainrod's real objective was to sicken me. It worked, of course, but once I cooled down I decided it would be in my best interests to avoid being pushed into asking away. I was too long in the tooth to fall for that one.

It was reserve football for me after that, although I did make two more first-team appearances that season when Paul Mathers was unavailable. Even so, there was to be no escape from controversy and I suffered another piece of character assassination when, through no fault of my own, I missed a game against Celtic's reserves in Glasgow. A mix-up over the time I was supposed to be picked up at a pre-arranged meeting place in Auchterarder had left me stranded there without any means of transport. After dropping me off in plenty of time at the pick-up point, Linda had driven my car to Perth to do some shopping. I phoned Dens Park to discover that in fact the coach had passed through Auchterarder half an hour ahead of schedule. That did not solve the problem but at least it confirmed that I was blameless. Assistant manager Jim Duffy gave me an understanding ear but not so Stainrod. He again took the opportunity to lambast me in print, claiming that I had refused to turn up for the game. As it turned out, I was completely absolved. But I was left with the feeling that some of the mud which had been thrown at my name by Stainrod might have stuck.

When I tackled him about his public accusation and demand for an apology from me, he simply shrugged it off as if it were a bit of a joke and a matter of no importance. I was left gritting my teeth and wondering how much more humiliation I could take from him. My stay at Dens Park, which seemed a great deal longer than it actually was, plunged me into the same feeling of despair I had experienced at Old Trafford. It seemed scarcely believable that it was happening all over again. With hindsight I knew I should never have agreed to move to Dundee in the first place. It had been a big mistake and had left me standing in what I recognised as football's equivalent of that famous Wild West establishment 'The Last Chance Saloon'. My next move had to be the right one or my career would be heading for oblivion.

I went on loan to Sheffield United during my spell in Dundee's reserves and it was after I returned to Scotland that I was contacted by Hibs assistant manager Andy Watson, a former Aberdeen team-mate. He wanted to know if I would be interested in joining him at Easter Road. Obviously I was, but I heard nothing more that summer and had actually completed a week of pre-season training with Dundee when Hibs manager Alex Miller contacted me. He told me everything had been arranged between the two clubs and that the way was now clear for me to join Hibs on a free transfer. I met Miller, as arranged, at a motorway service station between Perth and Edinburgh and quickly decided that this was the move I had been praying for. I was greatly impressed by the way the Hibs boss spoke about his plans for his club – and his obvious faith in me. When I signed for him in July 1993, I was determined to repay that faith. Miller deserved no less for he was the only top club boss who had shown interest in me after I was dropped by Stainrod.

He has since said that he did not regard taking me to Easter Road as a gamble, but I beg to differ. I might easily have lost any semblance of ambition after the set-backs I endured at Old Trafford and Dens Park. Only I knew what was going on inside my head. Happily, I was able to prove him right. In my first season at Easter Road I helped Hibs reach the final of the Skol League Cup and by November I was back in Scotland's team. Not bad going for an old reject. As you would expect, I took great satisfaction from two back-to-back wins over Dundee at the start of that first season. After knocking them out in the third round of the Skol Cup, we handed them a League defeat at the same venue, Easter Road, four days later. That first game was Stainrod's last as Dundee's manager, for he was then moved upstairs to become the club's director of football. Meanwhile, the two victories put a smile on my face for a week.

SEVEN

Happy with Hibs

S trange though it may seem, I enjoyed the autumn of my career much more than the spring or summer, and joining Hibs had a great deal to do with that. Despite my age – I was 35 when I arrived at Easter Road – and experience, it was a bit like starting all over again. Adversity had taught me to savour each game as if it were my last, and I'd like to think that Hibs benefited from that attitude and the enthusiasm I was able to rekindle with them. What I do know, for sure, is that in my four years with the Edinburgh club I produced the most consistent form of my life. Manager Alex Miller deserves a lot of the credit for that. His support and encouragement were crucial factors in my bid to put my career back on the rails. I was also motivated by the fear of letting down a man who had put his trust in me.

Happily, things could not have gone better for me in my first season with Hibs. In the early part of that campaign, we topped the Premier Division three times. Our progress in the Skol League Cup was another pleasing factor, and while we were disappointed by our defeat from Rangers in the final in October, 1993, it felt good to be back on such a stage. With Hampden unavailable because of reconstruction work, the final was played at Celtic Park. All my family and friends were there in the crowd of 47,362 and their presence meant a lot to me. It was, after all, my first final since Manchester United's draw with Crystal Palace at Wembley, and they had been involved in the bad times I had endured since then. I could never have climbed back to the top without them. I don't think Hibs had enough players who believed we could beat Rangers, but it took a super goal to give our opponents their victory. An own goal by Dave McPherson put us back on level terms after Ian Durrant had given Rangers the lead, but the ace up the Ibrox team's sleeve was Ally McCoist, who came on as a 67th-minute substitute for Pieter Huistra. McCoist, who broke his leg playing for Scotland in Portugal, had started in only two of Rangers' League matches prior to the final that season, but he scored one of the most spectacular winners I've ever seen. There was no chance of my saving his overhead kick just nine minutes from the end.

As you can imagine, McCoist has managed to remind me about that shot many times since and clearly enjoys doing so. He's got such a great personality that you would find it difficult to fall out with him, even when he is giving you a hard time. My own view of that final is that if Hibs had finished as well as they started, the outcome might have been very different. But let's not have any of that 'if only' stuff. I don't believe in making excuses for myself or my team.

I found Hibs a very friendly club and enjoyed a family atmosphere at Easter Road. A warm welcome awaited me when I arrived there and settling in was not a problem. Later, when I earned a Scotland recall, it seemed that everyone connected with Hibs was proud of what I had achieved. I was also fortunate to establish an early rapport with Hibs supporters. They sensed I was determined to do my best for their club and reacted accordingly.

When I left Hibs to return to Aberdeen in the summer of '97, the number of letters I received from the Edinburgh club's fans overwhelmed me. All of them wished me well at Pittodrie, and I appreciated that more than any of the praise I have been given either before or since. A player who packs his bags and joins a rival club is not always given such a friendly send off. Even more remarkable is that fact that Hibs fans still seemed well disposed towards me even when I was playing against their favourites. They always saved some of their cheers for me when I took the field. It's that sort of thing that restores your faith in human nature.

I played a total of 178 games for Hibs, and our best season during my stay with them was in our 1994–95 campaign. As well as finishing third in the Premier Division, we reached the semi-final of the Tennents Scottish Cup. Much to the delight of our support, we also put an end to a long-running hoodoo by beating Hearts 1–0 at Tynecastle in August. Gordon Hunter's goal broke a miserable run of 22 games against our Edinburgh rivals without a victory. We did not play well, but the fact that the jinx had been broken was a great boost for us and we enjoyed two more Premier Division wins over Hearts that season. Hibs had not won the Scottish Cup since 1902 – 93 years earlier – but Miller was convinced we could end our club's long wait that season. He talked us into feeling the same way, insisting that this would be the year we could make ourselves immortal in the eyes of our fans. It was not to be, however, for while we drew 0–0 with Celtic in our semi-final at Ibrox, they won the replay 3–1. My penalty save from Andy Walker had helped keep the score-sheet blank in the first game, but there was no stopping Celtic in the replay. Their goals came from Willie Falconer, John Collins and Phil O'Donnell while Keith Wright scored for us. Losing to Celtic was a huge disappointment because we felt we could have beaten Airdrie in the final. Having said that, the First Division club was good enough to eliminate Hearts in their semi-final at

Hampden. They also restricted Celtic to a 1-0 win in the final, with Pierre van Hooijdonk producing the winner, so perhaps we were kidding ourselves.

My worst season with Hibs – it was also my last – was in 1996–97, when we finished second bottom in the Premier Division table and were required to win a play-off with Airdrie in order to preserve our status. Thankfully, we defeated the Lanarkshire club 5–2 on aggregate and that was a huge relief. I would have hated to leave Hibs in the wake of their relegation. That was a black season for me in more ways than one, for Miller resigned as manager after we lost 3–1 to Hearts at Easter Road at the end of September. Jocky Scott then took over on a caretaker basis, but was sacked two months later. If Scott had kept the job, and all the players wanted him to, I would have been faced with a very tough decision. Such was my respect for him that I would have been tempted to stay with Hibs rather than move back to Aberdeen. My association with Scott goes back a long way, for we played together at the start of my first spell at Pittodrie. I rate his training methods very highly and second only to those of Archie Knox. As I've said, Scott was not short of admirers in our dressing-room. Had it been up to the players, he would have been given the manager's job on a permanent (if there is such a thing) basis. We were most unhappy about the way he was treated.

Jim Duffy left Dundee to become our new boss and made a spectacular arrival at Easter Road by helicopter. Despite the fact that Duffy had been Stainrod's assistant during my days of despondency at Dens Park, I held no grudge against him. But what I did not like was the direction in which Hibs headed following his appointment. I felt it would be in my best interests to move on, although at first I did not know where. That question was answered shortly after Duffy's arrival when Tommy Craig, Roy Aitken's assistant at Aberdeen, asked me if I would be interested in moving back to

Pittodrie. Obviously, the idea of rejoining my first club appealed to me – especially as I had enjoyed so much success with Aberdeen in the past. Our children had also been brought up in that city, so we still had strong links there. At the same time, the family enjoyed living in Auchterarder and I was concerned about Claire and Greg having to go through the hassle of changing schools at a vital stage in their education. I felt it would have been unfair of me to make any decision without consulting all the Leightons, so I took a vote. The verdict was unanimous. Everyone was in favour of moving back to the Granite City.

I had a discussion with Aitken after that and a deal was sorted out very quickly. In fact, I knew I would be rejoining Aberdeen on a free transfer long before that play-off with Airdrie. Settling my own future did not make me any less anxious about the uncertainty facing Hibs. As I've told you, I was desperate to leave the Edinburgh club where I had found them – in the top flight. Although his stay at Easter Road was brief, one of the players who made a big impression on me during my time with Hibs was former England midfielder Ray Wilkins. Wilkins, whose previous clubs included Rangers and Manchester United, signed for Hibs on a month-to-month basis prior to Miller's resignation. We did not see much of him because he did not link up with us until the Friday of each week after flying from London, but what an impact this splendid veteran had on our young players. All of them were desperate to show the hugely experienced and much-travelled Ray what they could do and, as a consequence, worked their socks off in training. It's fair to say that Ray's presence and great charm lifted all of us, and we were sorry when Jim Duffy let him go. Wilkins is the living proof that nice guys can be winners.

EIGHT

Four World Cup Finals

The World Cup has given me some of the worst, as well as the best, moments of my footballing life, but I count myself extremely fortunate to have played at that level. I've been involved in four final competitions, and that is one Scottish record that may never be broken. You have to be around the international scene for a very long time to produce that kind of statistic. I also find it a very humbling thought that some of the finest players my country has produced never once appeared on that stage. Remember that when Scotland qualified for the 1974 finals in what was then West Germany, it ended a long spell in the World Cup wilderness. Prior to that their last appearance had been in Sweden – 16 years earlier.

When Scotland manager Jock Stein, one of Scottish football's legendary figures, named me in his squad for the 1982 finals in Spain, I could hardly believe my luck. I was only 23 and had not yet made my debut at full international level. It was also a very pleasant surprise. Stein had previously told me he would not take me to Spain as an uncapped player, so I thought my chance of being included in his plans had gone. While he had talked about the possibility of bringing me on as a second-half replacement for Arsenal's George Wood in the British Championship match against Northern Ireland in Belfast, that did not happen. My heart sank when Stein spoke to Wood and I at Windsor Park on the day before the game. He said he had decided to field the Arsenal player because, as well as wanting to see what Wood could do, he was looking for a victory. 'If we are winning 3–0 with ten minutes to go, I might bring you on,' he told me. I was shattered by his words and, for the record, Scotland drew 1–1.

Against that background, you can imagine how pleased I was to find myself named in the squad of 22 players Stein took to Portugal to prepare for his campaign in Spain. It was the kind of news that takes time to sink in. There was I, the only rookie in Scotland's party, training in the Algarve sunshine and rubbing shoulders with famous names like Liverpool's Kenny Dalglish and Graeme Souness and Joe Jordan of AC Milan. As I had been involved at the top end of the professional game with Aberdeen for only four years, it was the steepest learning curve imaginable. But that was exactly what Stein wanted it to be. He explained that while he had no intention of fielding me in any of our World Cup finals group ties against New Zealand, Brazil and Russia, he wanted me to regard the trip as an educational one. I was to look, learn and soak up the atmosphere. Stein felt the experience of me being closely involved in Scotland's campaign would be of great benefit to me in the future and, of course, he was absolutely right. That did not prevent me from being in awe of some members of his squad. I was fortunate in that I had three Aberdeen team-mates – Willie Miller, Alex McLeish and Gordon Strachan – to help me settle in, but I have to say I had precious little assistance from some of the 'Anglos'.

Tottenham striker Steve Archibald, a former Pittodrie team-mate, was of course, an obvious exception, but some of the others were very clannish and kept to themselves. They formed a clique, the likes of which you would not find in later Scotland squads, and seemed to regard me as an interloper. For example, if I walked into the dining-room on my own, I was never invited to sit at the clique's table. It was a closed shop. Having said that, George Wood, understudy to first-choice goalkeeper Alan Rough, was absolutely brilliant to me. He knew the score and always made sure I had company. I won't forget his kindness or that of Strachan, who took me with him when he went to visit his family, after we had moved to Spain, at their hotel on the Costa Del Sol. One of the biggest lessons I learned during that campaign was how to occupy my time when I was not training or attending matches. We were not allowed to play golf or tennis at our Spanish headquarters at the Campo de Golf, Sotogrande, and sunbathing was also ruled out. Security was very tight, largely due to the terrorist threat, and we were not allowed out unless we were granted permission. Even then, we would be accompanied by security guards.

It was the first time I had been away from home for so long without members of my family, so at first I found it difficult to cope. I think it helped that, being an only child, I was used to being on my own, but that did not always enable me to handle boredom. It's entirely different when you know you are going to be involved in the action, for you can focus your mind on what lies ahead. That said, I now know Stein did me a massive favour by having me in the dressing-room prior to taking a seat in the stand at Scotland's matches. I did as he instructed, looking and learning as our players prepared to step out on football's global stage, and it was an invaluable experience. We won our opening tie, against New Zealand in Malaga, 5–2. Despite the fact that our opponents provided us with some awkward moments, it was the winning start we required. The first game in a World Cup finals group is always crucial and, as we Scots know to our cost, losing it can shove you in the direction of an early exit from the competition.

Although I was really more of a supporter than a player in Spain, I was as nervous as I have ever been before a big game when we travelled to Seville for our next match against mighty Brazil in the Benito Villamarin stadium. I also remember how it felt when I stepped out of the team coach into a wall of heat. In fact, even during the evening of the match the temperature was not far short of 100 degrees, and sitting in the stand was like being in a sauna. Obviously the conditions favoured the Brazilians, but Scotland got off to a marvellous start when Dundee United's Dave Narey cracked a great shot high into the net in the 18th minute. Jimmy Hill's derisive description of that effort as a 'toe poke' earned him the undying emnity of Scotland fans. More importantly, however, the shot roused Brazil's stars to such an extent that they produced a four-goal reply. The irrepressible Strachan, who is never at a loss for words regardless of the circumstances, was later to ask Narey – 'Why did you do that? You only got them angry.'

Watching that game I could not help but admire the sublime skills of Brazilian stars like Zico, Falcao and Socrates, but it was sometimes difficult to concentrate on the play. You could not hear yourself speak because of the throbbing samba drums that seemed to set the rhythm for our opponents and it was like being in the middle of a huge party. Brazil's fans sang and danced around me as they celebrated each of their team's goals, and you had to smile at their uninhibited joy. I felt I needed a souvenir of the occasion and exchanged jerseys with Brazil's third goalkeeper after the game. It is something I still treasure along with the memory of an amazing night in Seville. Stein was not at all happy with Alan Rough's display against Brazil and wasted no time in conveying his feelings to his assistant, Dundee United manager Jim McLean. He told the Tannadice boss that Rough would not play again for Scotland as long as he was manager. Stein said that, despite my inexperience, I would be promoted above both Rough and Wood and play in our last group tie against Russia in Malaga. McLean, who told me about the situation later, managed to talk Stein out of dropping Rough, arguing that it would be extremely unfair on me to make my Scotland début in a match we had to win in order to stay in the competition. I would have loved to play in that tie, of course, but I think McLean was right. Facing Russia in such a vital encounter could have killed off my international career before it had even started. A late goal by Souness in Malaga's Estadio La Rosaleda earned Scotland a 2–2 draw, but of course it wasn't enough to keep us in Spain. All I knew, as I watched our World Cup dream evaporate in the sunshine, was that I was desperate to be involved in my country's next bid for glory in this tournament.

On the flight home I sat beside a journalist I knew and trusted. 'It will be your turn next,' he said. Prophetic words indeed. It was four months later that I earned my first cap in a European Championship qualifying tie against East Germany at Hampden which produced a 2–0 victory for Scotland. I felt I was on my way at last, and keeping a clean sheet seemed a good way to start. Scotland were back on the World Cup trail in what seemed like no time at all. Our qualifying rivals for the race to Mexico '86 were Iceland, Spain and Wales, and we were determined to make it four finals in a row. We got off to a flier, too, with a 3–0 win over Iceland at Hampden. Paul McStay scored two of our goals and Charlie Nicholas the other.

Spain came to Hampden the following month for what was obviously one of the crunch ties in our group and we produced a display worthy of the occasion. Looking back on that 3–1 win I now rate it as probably the finest performance by any of the Scotland teams in which I figured. Mo Johnston scored twice and Kenny Dalglish topped off a great night with one of the best goals I've ever seen. The next tie was also against Spain, in Seville, and I'll never forget that evening in the Ramon Sanchez Pizjuan stadium. Spanish fans made me the target for a non-stop bombardment of oranges, beer bottles and loaves of bread. Some of the missiles were hurled from a great height and landed in my goalmouth with considerable force. I had to ask the French referee, Michel Vautrot, to stop the game three times in order to have the debris cleared away and bring about a temporary cease-fire. On one occasion the barrage was so heavy that I felt obliged to run out of my goal and past one of my defenders, Willie Miller, to tell the French official that I was in danger of being seriously hurt. The Spanish fans behind my goal were very close to me, for I had to stand against the moat wall in order to take my goal-kicks. Turning my back on that crowd was not a pleasant feeling, and I half expected to be struck by a missile as I did so. Happily, that did not happen, but the hostility did not end after Spain's 1–0 victory. The fans poked sticks at us as we walked through a police cordon to get to our coach and Steve Archibald had to come to our rescue.

Steve, then with Barcelona, was a Spanish football hero and the fans treated him with respect. He must have made that journey to and from the coach eight times as he escorted other members of Scotland's squad to safety. Despite all that, the atmosphere during the game was something special. I don't think I've played in a more electrifying scene. Wales at Hampden was the next test and their 1–0 victory was a major set-back for us. An Ian Rush goal was responsible for handing me my first home defeat since coming into the Scotland team. We headed for Iceland after a Richard Gough goal had given us a 1–0 victory over England at Hampden in the Rous Cup and, of course, that result boosted our confidence. I was looking forward to helping Scotland gather more World Cup points in Reykjavik, although we were well aware of Iceland's marked improvement in international football. Everything went well until the day before the tie when I was injured in training. David Speedie came in to challenge me for the ball and I sailed over the top of him to land head first. I felt something happen to my neck muscles and found I could not straighten my head. I could not even look to my right without experiencing excruciating pain. The doctor gave me some pills and sent me to bed, but even there I found no escape from my discomfort. I could not rest my head on the pillow.

By the morning of the match there was no improvement and it seemed certain that I would have to call off. I was given more pills and sent back to bed. This time, I managed to fall asleep, but got a shock when I woke up. I discovered my neck had gone so numb that I could not feel a thing. With hindsight, I should never have played in that tie, but I did and had one of the luckiest breaks of my life when Iceland were awarded a penalty. It was not a case of inspired judgement when I dived to my left and saved that spot kick. The simple fact is that I could never have flung myself in the other direction anyway. It turned out to be a vital save, for a Jim Bett goal four minutes from the end gave Scotland a 1–0 victory. I shudder to think what might have happened if Iceland had found out about my injury and aimed all their shots to my right.

The chips were down when we went into our last qualifying tie, against Wales in Cardiff, for we needed a draw to finish second in our group and so go into a play-off for a place in Mexico. That made it a tense, nervous build-up and no one seemed under more pressure than Stein. Our manager was like an angry bear, and everyone felt the rough edge of his tongue as he led us towards the action. Little did we then know that the strain of steering Scotland through this tie would be too much for him and prove fatal. Having beaten Scotland in Glasgow, Wales were up for the Cardiff showdown and the bustling Mark Hughes put them ahead in the 13th minute. Ten minutes later, I went for a cross with Robbie James and found myself in dire straits. The Welshman's pinkie had dragged across my face and knocked my contact lens out of my left eye. My frantic search of my goalmouth failed to locate the missing lens and I cannot describe the panic I was in for the rest of the first half. I soon discovered that, with only one lens, I could no longer judge distances or the flight of the ball. I was extremely fortunate not to lose a goal when, on one occasion, the ball bounced off my leg after I had completely misread its proximity to me. That was by no means the only close call, either. It was, without doubt, the longest 22 minutes of my life.

When half time arrived I was given a roasting by my Aberdeen boss, Alex Ferguson, who was Stein's assistant. Like the rest of the Scotland players, he could not understand what had gone wrong with me. I was frightened to tell him the truth, for I'd kept the fact that I wore lenses a closely guarded secret. Even he, my club manager, did not know. I made straight for the dressing-room toilet, hoping against hope that the missing lens might have become lodged under my eyelid. It wasn't there, however, and an examination by Celtic physiotherapist Brian Scott confirmed that. It was time to own up, for I knew there was no way I could go back out on that Ninian Park pitch. To make matters worse, I also had to confess that I had left my spare pair of lenses at home in Aberdeen! Understandably, Ferguson could not believe his ears when I told him my tale of woe. He must have felt embarrassed as well as angry. Stein's reaction to my news was different. He turned ashen-faced before storming away without saying a word.

Sadly, it turned out to be the last time I saw him alive.

Alan Rough, the most laid-back character imaginable, took my place in goal after the interval and you had to admire his nonchalant style. He trotted out as if he was heading for a bounce game in a public park rather than a vital World Cup tie which was on a knife edge. I could not bear to watch the rest of the game and sat, out of sight, on a hamper in the toilet while a security man gave me updates on the state of play. I heard the roar when Davie Cooper equalised for Scotland from the penalty spot with nine minutes to go and I have never felt more relieved than when I learned that we had drawn 1–1. That feeling did not last, however, because I also heard that Stein had collapsed in the Scotland dug-out and been carried to the medical room. He died shortly afterwards, plunging an entire nation into mourning.

I'll never forget the white faces of the Scotland fans as they digested the shock news after the game. They should have been celebrating an important result, but none of them were and it was in an emotional silence that our players left the ground. Scotland had lost one of its great heroes. In the wake of the Cardiff tragedy, Ferguson agreed to take over the duties of national team boss and combine them with his club job.

Scotland needed to prepare for a two-leg play-off with Australia, winners of the World Cup's Oceania group, and Stein's assistant was the obvious choice to fill the managerial void. A preparatory game against East Germany at Hampden saw Ferguson begin his reign with a 0–0 draw. Andy Goram won his first cap in that game when he replaced me at half-time. Australia came to the same venue the following month for the first leg of the play-off and we required no motivation for that tie. We wanted to win for Big Jock, as well as ourselves, for we all felt indebted to him. He had been at Scotland's helm for 61 matches. Goals by Davie Cooper and Frank McAvennie gave us a 2–0 lead to carry to Australia, but we knew were going to have to battle to preserve that advantage. The Australians were a big, physical side and quite capable of putting us under pressure in their own backyard. That was how it turned out, for we had to put in a lot of hard work in defence to keep them at bay in a match which finished a no-score draw. It took us 28 hours to get to Australia for 90 minutes of football, but it was well worth the trouble. We were Mexico bound.

We went to Santa Fe to prepare for the heat and altitude problems we would have to contend with in Mexico and finished our build-up in Los Angeles. We felt ready for the group ties which awaited us in the '86 finals and looked forward to making a good start against Denmark in the Neza Stadium. In fact, our opening tie turned out to be a huge disappointment, for the Danes won an uneventful game 1–0 via a Preben Elkjaer goal. It was a fortuitous counter. The ball came off Willie Miller's shin as he went to tackle Elkjaer, and that left the Danish striker with the opportunity to beat me with a shot which went in off the post. Our next task in what had been dubbed 'The Group of Death' was against West Germany in Queretaro, and we knew we were up against it after losing to the Danes. In addition to the quality in Franz Beckenbauer's team, the Queretaro tie had a midday kick-off. With the lunchtime temperature around 100 degrees, there was no way we could sustain an up-and-at-'em style. Weighed before and after that tie, I know that I lost 8lbs. I shudder to think what some outfield players must have shed.

Although the German team was packed with big names, we surprised them by opening the scoring through Strachan in the 18th minute. It was a magnificent goal and Gordon's sense of humour was to the fore as he celebrated by lifting his leg on top of an advertising hoarding. He was letting the crowd know that, unlike other World Cup scorers, he was too small to jump over. The Germans wiped the smile from our faces only five minutes later when Voller equalised. Allofs then scored their second five minutes after the break and they toyed with us for the rest of the second half. We went into our last group tie, against Uruguay, knowing we had to win to stay in Mexico – a familiar scenario. We were also, or so we thought, well prepared for the bully-boy tactics of the South Americans. I got my first taste of Uruguay's repertoire of dirty tricks before the game had even started. Goram and I were warming up when the entire Uruguayan squad came on and made a bee-line for our end of the pitch. They then proceeded to hammer balls at me as hard as they could, pausing only to shake their fists in my face. I kicked one of their balls into the crowd and thought for a moment that I was going to be lynched. It was at that point that Goram and I decided discretion was the better part of valour and left the scene in some haste.

Far worse was to follow in the match itself. Strachan was immediately targeted for rough-house treatment, and a dreadful foul on him by Jose Batista in the first 60 seconds led to the Uruguayan being sent off. Did that discourage the South Americans? Not a bit. They carried on biting, scratching and kicking our players, Strachan in particular, all over the pitch. Corner kicks were a nightmare, for they spat in your face and pulled hairs out of your arms. Having sent off Batista so early in the game, the French referee seemed reluctant to punish the Uruguayans any further, so they got away with murder. Neither did he add any stoppage time. If he had, the tie would have lasted an extra 20 minutes. SFA officials were furious after the 0–0 draw, with secretary Ernie Walker referring to the Uruguayans as 'scum', but that did not, of course, change anything. We had lost a great chance to progress beyond the first stage of the finals and it was time to go home. Back in the dressing-room I could hardly believe that some members of our squad were actually quite happy about our failure. All they were interested in was going on holiday. I wanted to bang their heads against the wall until they shed tears like the ones in my eyes.

Ferguson moved from Aberdeen to Manchester United five months after our Mexico campaign. Scotland's new team boss, SFA Director of Coaching, Andy Roxburgh, already had games under his belt by then, and the big question was whether he could lead his country to the World Cup finals in Italy, thus making it five in a row. Qualification for the biggest football show on earth was becoming a habit. Our qualifying group rivals were Norway, Yugoslavia, France and Cyprus and you did not have to be a football expert to appreciate that finishing in one of the top two places in that group would be no easy task. Scotland's opening tie was against Norway in Oslo in September, 1988, four months after I had followed Ferguson from Pittodrie to Old Trafford, and we produced a good performance. The Norwegians were making rapid strides in improving their international status and we did well to win 2-1 with goals from Paul McStay and Mo Johnston. An away victory, especially in the first match, can be the key to qualifying success, so we were delighted with our start. It meant that we went into our next test, at the hands of a formidable Yugoslavian team at Hampden, with something in the bag. I missed that tie because of an injury I sustained at Perth the previous day. In fact, our training session was over when I kicked a ball away and tore a muscle in my back. I did not see the match – a 1-1 draw – because I was ordered to return to Manchester immediately for treatment. But I was told that my replacement, Andy Goram, had done well. Johnston was our scorer.

I was back in Scotland's goal for the game against Cyprus in Limassol in February, 1989, and what a nail-biting affair that turned out to be on a terrible pitch. It did not help matters when I dropped a corner and Cyprus profited from my mistake to score their second goal, but we somehow managed to fight our way to a 3-2 win. Richard Gough, who scored twice, was our Limassol hero, his second goal coming in the sixth minute of stoppage time. Talk about a close call. Cypriot fans were infuriated by that later-than-late winner and rioted after the final whistle. We heard the thumps and bangs as they tried to break into the East German referee's room. It wasn't too pleasant for us, either, for we required police assistance to get to our dressing-room. The referee was later smuggled to the airport. Without doubt, we were very fortunate to snatch victory from that tie. In the circumstances, it was one heck of a result.

Any chance of there being a calm, unhurried approach to our next tie, against France at Hampden in March, went out of the window when we got stuck in a traffic jam on the way from our Gleneagles Hotel headquarters. Without the help of police outriders we would never have got to the game on time. As it was, we arrived just 30 minutes before kick-off. Heavy rain made it a dreadful night for the fans, but Scotland's team put a spring in squelching shoes by turning in a storming display. This time it was Mo Johnston's turn to be a two-goal hero in our 2–0 win, and the fact that he was then playing for French club Nantes added piquancy to his contribution. He also suffered heavy punishment at the hands of France's defenders.

After gathering seven out of eight points, Scotland made it nine out of ten by beating Cyprus 2–1 at Hampden. Johnston and Ally McCoist scored our goals in a game in which the Cypriots staged a football version of the Alamo. It was a frustrating night for us, as well as our supporters, but as I've said before it is results, rather than performances, that are remembered. We lost our unbeaten record in Yugoslavia in September, 1989, managing to concede two own goals on the way to a 3–1 defeat in Zagreb. I was at fault with the first goal, failing to beat Srecko Katanec to a cross, but I've no wish to make our mistakes detract from Yugoslavia's excellent performance. They were a fantastic side and showed it after Gordon Durie had put us in front. France took their revenge on us in Paris a month later, with a fellow named Eric Cantona running riot. In his team-talk prior to the game, Roxburgh had made it clear that he did not rate Cantona, describing him as 'a poor man's Joe Jordan', but the bold Eric was the man who pulled the strings in his team's 3–0 victory. He also scored one of his team's goals. Despite our reverses in Zagreb and Paris, we went into our last game against Norway at Hampden in November needing only a point to ensure that we finished second to group leaders Yugoslavia and clinched our place in Italy '90.

It was another of those nervy occasions, even though McCoist put us in front just before the break, and I was bitterly disappointed when Norway scored an equaliser in injury time – especially as Erland Johnsen's shot was hit from 40 yards. I was convinced the ball was heading past the post when it suddenly took a tremendous bend. I've never seen anything like it before or since, for it must have moved in the air a good four yards before leaving me looking badly at fault as it went into the net. Fortunately that freakish goal was of no consequence, but it certainly annoyed me and took the shine off my qualifying celebrations. My Wembley woe with Manchester United made me more determined than ever to give Scotland my very best in Italy. I flung myself into our preparations in Malta and trained like a man possessed. Despite Roxburgh's public declaration of his faith in me as his No. 1 goalkeeper, I felt it would be a close call between Goram and myself for that role in the finals. In fact, it was only three days before our opening tie against Costa Rica in Genoa that I knew, for sure, I would be playing in that game.

I thought we made a big mistake in that tie, which Costa Rica won 1–0, by showing them far too much respect. Rather than going straight for the jugular, we allowed them time to settle and gain confidence by stringing passes together. I honestly believe that had we produced a typical Scottish performance we would have wiped the floor with them. In any event, a Juan Cayasso goal was enough to separate the teams and earn us, with considerable justification, the wrath of our support.

We had to win our next tie in Genoa, against Sweden, and this time there was no more of the Mr Nice Guy nonsense. It's no exaggeration to say that some of the Swedish players turned pale when they saw the aggressive mood we were in. We growled and glared in the tunnel before the match and, in the first five minutes, threatened to sweep our opponents off the pitch. We won every tackle, flattening Swedes in the process, and were breathing fire. Stuart McCall gave us an early lead, in the tenth minute, and a late penalty, from which Johnston scored, proved to be the clincher. Sweden hit back with a Glenn Stromberg goal four minutes from the end, but we held firm. I still smile when I recall our penalty, awarded when Roy Aitken was brought down, for it was one of the worst dives I've seen. Big Roy was a warrior and a great man to have in your team, but no ballet dancer. That victory helped us recover from the numbing experience of the Costa Rica defeat and regain some credibility. It also lifted some of the pressure from Roxburgh's shoulders. One of the banners held aloft before the Sweden game said it all – 'Andy, your P45 is in the post.'

We needed a draw in our last group tie against Brazil in Turin to stay in the competition, and I have to say I don't think we handled the situation well. We were in complete awe of their players and their famous yellow jerseys, yet this was a very ordinary Brazil compared with some of their super-teams of the past. There was no need for us to be as negative as we were in the Stadio Nuovo Delle Alpi. Despite that, we were on level terms with only eight minutes to go when a shot from Alemao bounced in front of me and came off the ground very quickly. It then hit me and broke away to create a scramble. I thought one of our defenders might have managed to come to the rescue, but it was not to be and Muller profited from the situation to score the only goal of the game. I was blamed for the loss of that goal and offer no excuses. It was a goalkeeping error that had opened the door for Brazil and it took me a long time to get over it. I stayed on the pitch after the final whistle. The thought in my mind was that this would be my last appearance in the World Cup finals. As well as dwelling on my error, I wanted to look around me and remember what playing at that level had been like. The Brazilian goalkeeper, Claudio Taffarel, came all the way from the other end of the pitch to console me. He spoke very little English and I had no Portuguese, but we understood each other perfectly. Only another goalkeeper knows how lonely you can feel in such circumstances, and I much appreciated his gesture. I'd made one mistake in three games. But it was one too many. I've never forgotten Taffarel's kindness and was delighted for him when he picked up a winners' medal in the 1994 finals in America.

My Old Trafford troubles led to my disappearance from the international scene after that Turin defeat. There seemed no way back for me, especially when my move to Dundee did further and perhaps irreparable damage to my reputation. Indeed, by the time Alex Miller signed me for Hibs in the summer of 1993, I was convinced that my Scotland days were over. Miller, however, did not agree. He told me he wanted to see me back in Scotland's squad within six months of my arrival at Easter Road. I welcomed his vote of confidence but told my new boss I was not even considering the possibility of a Scotland recall. I said that my priorities lay elsewhere. I wanted to concentrate all my thoughts on re-establishing myself at the top level in club football and producing my best form for Hibs.

It came as a big surprise when Miller was proved right – and well within the deadline he had set for me. What happened was that two goalkeepers – Bryan Gunn and Alan Main – had to call off from new team boss Craig Brown's squad for a World Cup match in Malta – the last tie in Scotland's unsuccessful bid to reach America in '94. The withdrawals gave rise to speculation that, because of my club form, I might be in line for a comeback. It also sparked a lively debate in the Leighton household. Linda said she did not fancy the idea of me being recalled for a game Scotland would be expected to win because I would be on a hiding to nothing. She also told me, in no uncertain fashion, that she did not want us to go through another trauma. That was the state of the party when the phone rang in our Auchterarder home one night as we were having dinner with Dundee goalkeeper Paul Mathers and his wife. It was Alex Miller, Brown's assistant, confirming that, as forecast, there was a place for me in Scotland's squad. In view of Linda's reservations, I said I'd have to talk things over with my wife before giving my answer. She knew, however, that I wanted to accept the chance, and gave her blessing. I never did manage to finish my meal that night! My recall was a great boost for our children, as well as myself. They could not wait to tell their class-mates at Auchterarder High School that their father was back in business as a Scotland player and heading for Malta. They had put up with a great deal of hassle when I was being branded a failure, so they also enjoyed reading some positive comments about me in the newspapers. It is a true saying that you never fully appreciate what you have until you lose it. That is why pulling on a Scotland jersey in Malta, where we won 2–0, was such a marvellous feeling for me. It was nearly three and a half years since I'd last played for my country in Turin and that made the moment even sweeter.

Another interesting statistic was my lack of first-team action at club level during that period. I played only 21 League games for Dundee and, by the time I went to Malta, had made only 17 League appearances for Hibs. Brown, who first took over from Roxburgh on a caretaker basis, had his Scotland role confirmed before the Malta tie. It was not until we were in the dressing-room prior to the match that SFA president Bill Dickie gave us official notice of the appointment. At that time I did not think my service under Brown would last more than one game, but I was again proved wrong. Goram was in goal for the start of Scotland's bid to qualify for the '98 World Cup finals in France. I was on the bench when we drew 0–0 in Austria and beat Latvia 2–0, with John Collins and Darren Jackson our scorers in Riga. My chance came in the third tie against Sweden at Ibrox in November 1996, when Goram was injured, and

I felt I had something to prove. It put an extra edge on my preparations, as did the fact that I would be earning my 75th cap. In fact, things could not have gone better for me. Although I say it myself, it was probably one of my best displays for Scotland. It certainly earned me a great deal of praise after a John McGinlay goal gave us a 1-0 victory. Goram was back for our 0-0 draw with Estonia in Monaco, but I played in the remaining six ties. We had 2-0 wins over Estonia at Kilmarnock and Austria at Celtic Park before being beaten 2-1 by Sweden in Gothenburg. We then finished up with away and home wins over Belarus (1-0 in Minsk and 4-1 at Aberdeen) and a 2-0 victory against Latvia at Celtic Park. I lost only three goals in seven ties, and two of them were conceded at Gothenburg's Ullevi Stadium, scene of Aberdeen's European Cup-Winners' Cup triumph. The away win over Belarus in June, 1997, when a Gary McAllister penalty gave us victory, was my last game for Scotland as a Hibs player. My transfer back to Aberdeen was supposed to go through before that but Hibs chairman Douglas Cromb was very keen for me to represent the Easter Road club in that tie. He was far too nice a man to disappoint.

By happy coincidence, the next Scotland game – also against Belarus – was at Pittodrie in September. It meant a lot to me to play for Scotland there, which I did. It was also only the second time that Brown had been obliged to make a straight choice between Goram and myself. Kevin Gallacher and David Hopkin both scored twice in that win. While Austria topped our table, Scotland's 2-0 win over Latvia in Glasgow (Gallacher and Durie) secured qualification by virtue of us having the best record of all the second placed teams in the European groups. We were heading for France. In view of all that had happened to me since my last finals, eight years earlier, I felt like pinching myself. Such was the ticket frenzy sparked by our pairing with Brazil in the opening match of France '98 that I could have filled the Paris ground myself. Everywhere I went I was greeted with pleas for the precious briefs. One player, St Johnstone's Roddy Grant, actually asked me if I had any spare tickets during a match.

Due to the build-up to our meeting with Brazil, it was a relief to see the back of the domestic season. The tension kept mounting, just the same, as we prepared in America, and by then we could not wait to get to grips with our task in Paris. I found myself being affected by the long wait when we trained on the Stade de France pitch the day before the game. I was hopeless and could not catch a thing. As I've told you at the start of this book, all kinds of daft thoughts spring into your mind before a big game, and Paris gave me quite a few. On the morning of the match my head was in a whirl. I was so uptight that I wondered whether I would be able to handle the occasion. Strange though it may seem, all my self-doubts were swept away when I started to put on my kilt after lunch. It had been arranged that Scotland's squad would wear the kilt when they took a pre-match bow in Paris, and I can tell you that the historical significance of our national dress was certainly not lost on me. It put my head up and my chest out. It also motivated me more than any rousing team-talk. I'll confess that I had a lump in my throat when I stepped on the pitch in that kilt, and I know the fans loved the team's contribution to the colourful scene in the stadium.

I thought we handled the game well despite Brazil's Sampaio giving his team an early lead from a free header. We showed we had the appetite to cope with adversity when we recovered from that blow, and we worked hard for our equaliser which came from a John Collins penalty kick in the 38th minute. It was no more than we deserved. Brazil got their winner via a Tom Boyd own goal, but no blame can be attached to the Celtic defender. The ball cannoned off him in the 74th minute after I had blocked a shot and there was nothing he could do about it. Once again, the yellow jerseys had put us to the sword. We went to Bordeaux for our next tie, against Norway, and should have had more to show for our efforts than a 1–1 draw. We gave everything we had but could not put the ball in the net until Craig Burley's 66th-minute equaliser.

Linda's health was a big worry before the Norway tie. She had discovered a lump in her breast and I was in America when she began having tests. I had tried, without success, to contact her on the day of the Norway match, but just as I was leaving my hotel room the phone rang. The news was good. She had been given the all-clear and, as you can image, I felt that a weight had been lifted from my shoulders.

Colin Calderwood broke his wrist against Norway and his absence from our defence for the last group tie against Morocco in St Etienne was a big loss. Along with Colin Hendry and Tom Boyd, he had formed a stout trio at the back. Morocco were supposed to be Scotland's weakest rivals in France, but someone forgot to tell them that as Bassir put them in the lead after 23 minutes and I take full responsibility for their second goal, scored by Hadda. It was, quite simply, an avoidable and embarrassing blunder. There was no way back for us after that, and Bassir made it 3–0 five minutes from the end.

This time it really was my last appearance in the World Cup finals, but let me finish by clearing up some misconceptions about the 'fortunes' Scotland players make by appearing on that stage. By the time I paid for my tickets and phone calls, I was left with a balance of less than £200 from my earnings in France. On top of that it cost me £1500 to take my family there. Not that I grudged the Leighton family's trip to Paris . . . it was worth every penny. But I think these statistics prove I was much more interested in the honour of representing my country than any financial gain.

I believe it is right and proper that professional players should be suitably rewarded for stepping on the international stage, especially one as big as the World Cup, but cash was never a motivating factor for me when I pulled on a Scotland jersey in the finals. I know I could not have tried harder to please if I had been offered a bonus the size of a bumper win on the lottery, and I'm sure the vast majority of my former team-mates could make the same claim. It was pride, both national and personal, plus the fear of letting down Scotland's supporters, that spurred me throughout all my World Cup campaigns. While there were times when I should have done better, it certainly wasn't for lack of commitment to my country's cause. That was the crumb of comfort I took home from France, where we again failed to reach the second stage of the finals. I can assure you that no matter how much money I had been paid, it would never have compensated for the disappointment I felt there.

NINE.

Why I Quit Scotland's Squad

Playing for Scotland has been a privilege, as well as an honour, and I did not decide to end my international career without a great deal of heart-searching. It hurt when some people branded me a traitor for quitting Craig Brown's squad, so I welcome this opportunity to explain the real reason for my sudden retirement from international football after such long service in my country's colours. Contrary to popular belief, my decision was not precipitated by a fall-out with Scotland's boss. Indeed, nothing could be further from the truth. When I told him of my decision to retire and concentrate on playing for Aberdeen, I could not have had a more sympathetic hearing. He also did his level best to persuade me to stay in his squad and, as a consequence, move closer to my dream of making 100 international appearances. So why did I deny myself the possibility of making that dream come true? Quite simply because of one man – Scotland goalkeeping coach Alan Hodgkinson. But for him, I would have carried on playing for my country for as long as my services were required. It would be an understatement to say that my relationship with this former England player was not a good one.

So badly had our relationship deteriorated that, prior to my retirement, we had not spoken to each other for years. He had long since stopped wishing me luck before a game and our enmity was like a festering sore. To be blunt, I simply did not rate his coaching methods or enjoy working with him – and he knew it. I had felt, for a considerable length of time, that I was not getting any of the specialised work I needed during the build-ups for Scotland's matches. As a consequence, I felt under-prepared. It could have happened much earlier, but it was the dreadful atmosphere between Hodgkinson and myself before Scotland's European Championship qualifying tie against Estonia at Tynecastle on 10 October 1998, that led to me quitting. You could have cut it with a knife. As well as being unhappy with my preparations for that match, I began questioning the sense of me continuing to be a member of Brown's squad. Thanks to Hodgkinson, the fun had gone out of my involvement in international football and because of the way I felt about the goalkeeping coach, I did not see it returning. Those were the thoughts that were going through my mind as I stood in the line-up before the tie at Tynecastle, and it was Estonia's second goal, giving them a 2–1 lead, which hammered the final nail in my international coffin. There and then, I decided this would be my last game for Scotland.

As far as I was concerned, the fact that we went on to win 3–2 changed nothing, and my mind was in a turmoil as I travelled home to Aberdeen that night. On one hand I felt tempted to make just one more appearance because Scotland's next tie was against the Faroe Islands at Pittodrie – my home ground – the following Wednesday. Yet I also wondered whether, in my state of mind, this might turn out to be one game too many. A bridge too far, so to speak. By that Saturday night only my family and close friends knew I was poised to quit. Alex Miller, my club boss and Craig Brown's assistant, was away on family business and I could not get in touch with him. Jim Stewart, the Aberdeen and Scotland Under-21 goalkeeping coach, was one of the few who knew of my intention. He tried his best to talk me out of retiring but I knew, in my heart, that I was no longer looking forward to playing for my country. That said, my stomach was still churning on the Sunday because I was well aware of the fact that making my decision public was not going to be easy. Until then, representing Scotland had always given me a deep sense of satisfaction. It had also been a large part of my life and not something I could toss away like a pair of old boots. I needed time on my own to sort out the thoughts in my head and made for the beach with only our two Lhasa Apso dogs, Smudge and Parker, as company. While they chased each other across the sand, I made up my mind that my Scotland days were over. I told Brown of my decision when I met up with Scotland's squad in Aberdeen that night. It was an emotional experience for me, but he was well aware of the hostility between Hodgkinson and myself and was most understanding.

At the same time, he tried hard to change my mind and our conversation must have lasted an hour. There was no animosity between us. Quite the opposite, in fact, and our meeting ended with Scotland's boss advising me to go home and sleep on my decision. I appreciated Brown's attitude, but it did not change anything. As my roller-coaster experiences at club level would suggest, I'm the stubborn type. If I think I have made the correct decision I'll stick with it through thick and thin. That did not prevent me from being upset when I again met up with Brown on the Monday. I was choking on my words when I told him my decision stood. His last question was to ask me if I would stay with him if he changed the goalkeeping coach, but I told him I was not in the business of creating an opening for a friend such as Jim

Stewart. We parted friends. He went off to attend a press conference at which there would be at least one unexpected item of news on the agenda, while I took the dogs for another walk. I suspect I was not very lively company for Smudge and Parker on that occasion, either.

All hell was let loose after I returned from that walk and the scene outside our house was reminiscent of my post-Wembley siege. Having been given official confirmation of my retirement, the media were out in force to hear Leighton's side of the story. Business cards containing cash offers for an 'exclusive' were thrust through the letter box of our house and my daughter, Claire, found herself being jostled by a scrum of reporters and photographers as she came out to collect the dogs from me. I did not want to make public my reason for quitting. So I decided to make myself scarce.

With the help of a local hotel owner, who gave me temporary refuge, I then took a circuitous route home and, for the second time in my life, had to call on the police to clear people from my door. I know the media have a job to do, but there are times when some of them get carried away by their own enthusiasm. There were some hysterical reactions to my sudden retirement. Apart from being branded a traitor, there was a suggestion that I should never again be allowed to attend a Scotland game. It was a load of nonsense, but it hurt just the same. After earning 91 caps, I thought I should have been allowed to depart the international scene with some dignity. Instead, it seemed to me that I was being metaphorically tarred and feathered.

Ironically, Hodgkinson and I were once on very good terms. He was Manchester United's goalkeeping coach during my time with them and I found him supportive when my Old Trafford dreams crumbled and turned to dust. Later, when I was back in Scotland and learned that he had suffered a heart attack, I made regular phone calls to the hospital and his wife, Brenda, to check on his

TOP (INSET): Was this three-year-old preparing for the coming of the pass-back rule?

ABOVE: Skinny Jim as a teenager, taking part in a penalty shoot-out at Johnstone Burgh's ground

RIGHT: A 1980 pre-season photo

Voted Don of the Year by local newspaper readers. Gordon Strachan (left) and Willie Miller are in attendance

It's all about bottle. Eric Black and Neale Cooper help me show off my Player of the Month prize

In the wars again with an eye injury

A hair-raising save in my home League début against Morton in 1978

TOP: **Punching my weight against Rangers**

ABOVE: **Celebrating the clinching of my
first League championship at Tynecastle**

Saluting a goal – one
of my happy
moments with
Manchester United

LEFT: Tense moment as I prepare to face England

BELOW: Unfounded optimism after joining Dundee

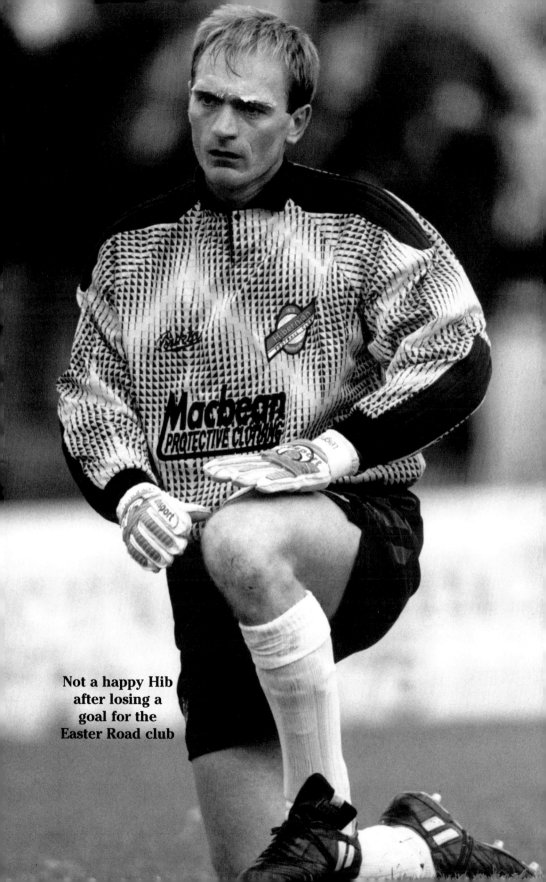

Not a happy Hib after losing a goal for the Easter Road club

LEFT: Hampden here we come . . . but my destination turned out to be the Victoria Infirmary

BELOW: With Middlesbrough manager Bryan Robson, a former Manchester United team-mate, at my testimonial match

progress. I can say, in all honesty, that it was no fault of mine when our relationship turned sour. The rot set in when Andy Goram – then with Rangers – and I were vying for the top goalkeeping job in Scotland's squad. I felt, and not without being given cause, that Hodgkinson's coaching duties with the Ibrox club influenced his thinking in terms of who should be Craig Brown's first choice. Neither was I happy with his training, which followed the same pattern every day and, in my view, was clearly designed to cater for Goram's needs rather than any of mine.

The situation came to a head in America during our preparations for the European Championship finals in England in 1996. As a big debate raged over the respective claims of Andy and myself, I was content to let my record speak for itself. I had played in the last six qualifying ties without conceding a goal. I had also been Scotland's first choice for a considerable length of time dating back to March 1995, when we drew with Russia in Moscow's Central Luzhniki Stadium. In the qualifying tie prior to that one, against Greece in Athens in December, 1994, I had replaced an injured Goram during the second half. Rightly or wrongly, I remain convinced that Hodgkinson played a key role in tipping the scales in Goram's favour for the finals. It was, of course, the national team boss who made the decision, but I knew the goalkeeping coach must have been asked for his views and that he would have done me no favours. He had said some 'iffy' things about me in newspaper interviews. He also knew I had not been slow to criticise him. When Craig told me that Andy would play in England, I was bitterly disappointed. There and then, I decided I would retire from international football.

Later, when I calmed down and was in a more receptive mood, Linda and my father talked me out of doing anything hasty. I'm glad they did, for I was able to make a pleasing comeback in the World Cup qualifying tie against Sweden at Ibrox in November

1996, which we won 1–0. That did not, however, change my view of Hodgkinson. The feedback I continued to receive from trusted sources within the Scotland camp was that he had very little that was good to say about me. If that sounds paranoid, then let me tell you about the kind of remarks which filtered back to me. On one occasion Alex Miller, my club boss, was informed by Hodgkinson that I trained and played like an old man and that Hibs should be looking for a new goalkeeper for the coming season. It wasn't only Alex he told, either. Hibs goalkeeping coach John Ritchie and Aberdeen goalkeeping coach Jim Stewart were both present when Hodgkinson delivered his verdict on me. Naturally, I wasted no time in confronting Hodgkinson about this insulting remark, but he denied being its author. On another occasion, Hodgkinson advised Craig Brown that I did not want to play in a friendly match against France in St Etienne and I was called to the manager's room to explain myself. I told him my refusal was news to me. I also said I thought he knew me better than that. Craig agreed that it had seemed completely out of character for me to turn down the chance to play for my country. By that time, however, the manager had already selected his team and, acting on information received, had left me out of it. Neil Sullivan had been given the job, with Andy on the bench.

When Scotland went to America to prepare for the 1998 World Cup finals in France, I thought my training was hopeless. Nor was I willing to suffer in silence. I had a meeting with Alex Miller and laid it on the line. I told the assistant Scotland boss that unless my preparations were dramatically improved, I would step in and take the goalkeepers' training myself. I also said I would give it two days before taking action and that I was determined to stick to that deadline. Goram changed the situation the very next day when he quit Scotland's squad and flew home. At the time, he blamed the media spotlight on his life outside football for his decision to turn his back on international football, but he now claims there were other reasons. No matter, to me the most significant fact is that he knew – having been tipped off by Hodgkinson – that he would not be playing in the World Cup opener against Brazil in Paris. There was more hassle for me after France 98 when I heard that Hodgkinson was claiming I was at fault for all of the six goals we lost to Brazil, Norway and Morocco.

Now, I don't mind fair and constrictive criticism and I'll accept blame when I think I should have done better, but I thought that charge was well over the top. It stung me into writing an official letter of complaint – not the first one, incidentally – to Craig Brown. He said that he would sort the matter out before the next game, a Euro 2000 qualifying tie in Lithuania, but nothing happened. I could have lived with this kind of aggro if playing for Scotland had not been so important to me, but I've always been something of a perfectionist and the harshest judge of my performances for club and country. In the end, it was the feeling that my self-imposed standards were in danger of slipping that helped me resist the temptation to carry on playing for Scotland. I don't think, in view of my long service record for my country, that I can fairly be accused of jumping ship. After all, Goram twice quit Scotland's squad – the first time was prior to a European Championship qualifier against Greece at Hampden in 1995 – yet remains as popular as ever. I must say that I do not go along with the view that a player who rejects a Scotland call-up is entitled to a second or even third chance. I think it demeans the honour of being selected for the national squad, and if that sounds old-fashioned then I don't give a damn.

Despite availability problems, I think Craig Brown should stick to the 'bravehearts' who really want to play for Scotland rather than chase after reluctant heroes. I also think it sends out the wrong signal when the SFA go down that path. I wish my successor, Neil

Sullivan, the luck that every goalkeeper needs because I always regarded him as being the best of the pretenders to my throne. Having worked with him and studied his technique at close quarters, I know the Scotland gloves are on a pair of extremely capable hands.

TEN

Wembley Woe and the Auld Enemy

W embley has not been kind to me, and the disappointment I suffered with Manchester United is only part of the story. I tasted defeat in both of the games I played in there for Scotland in 1983 and 1988, and was on the substitutes' bench at this famous stadium when England beat us 2–0 in Euro 96. I also watched Arsenal and Sheffield United lose FA Cup semi-finals at Wembley during my loan spells with them. My marked lack of good fortune at this ground earned me an unwanted title. It was bestowed on me by Sheffield United manager Dave Bassett on the eve of his team's semi-final with local rivals Sheffield Wednesday. Bassett was obviously hoping I might be some kind of talisman when he asked me about the outcome of my previous visits to Wembley, so I don't think he enjoyed my tale of woe. United were beaten 2–1 and from then on I was known at Bramall Lane as 'Lucky Jim.'

My father was one of those Scots who saved up their cash to make the pilgrimage to Wembley every second year, yet I had never been there until I played in our 2–0 defeat in 1983. It was only my sixth cap, but playing in front of an 84,000 crowd was not the daunting experience it could have been if I had not figured in big games at home and abroad with Aberdeen. I recall being a bit disappointed with the atmosphere at Wembley, but perhaps I was expecting too much after having been brought up on the folklore of this game. Who but the Scots would still be referring to the 'Wembley Wizards' – the Scotland team that beat England 5–1 in their own backyard more than 70 years ago?

There is nothing magical about the statistics from my six games against England – won one, drawn two and lost three – but I enjoyed playing in these games. I also derived a great deal of satisfaction from that lone victory, a 1–0 win at Hampden in 1988, because it was the first time England had been beaten in Glasgow since 1976. That victory also gave us the Rous Cup. Despite that happy memory, you can count me out of any campaign to restore the oldest international fixture in the world to our football calendar. No matter how attractive the idea may seem to some people, I honestly believe that a return to regular meetings between Scotland and England could be a recipe for disaster. In the wake of what happened during Euro 2000, I'm chilled by the thought of the fan trouble we could have on both sides of the border if this fixture was to be revived. The rioting by so-called England supporters in Brussels and Charleroi shamed their country's colours, and I don't think that these morons would think twice about causing havoc at a big match between British neighbours. Indeed, if the government's latest crackdown on England's hooligan fans travelling abroad is successful, the stay-at-homes might welcome an opportunity to indulge themselves in some unpleasantness on their own doorstep. The last thing Scotland's fans need is to become involved with English thugs, because they have too much to lose. I'm talking about the reputation they have built for themselves in foreign parts as well-behaved and sporting visitors. When you've earned good conduct medals, I don't see any point in taking the risk of having them ripped off your chest by neighbours from hell.

Don't get me wrong, I'm sorry England's team has a fan problem that is refusing to go away. Nor do I feel smug about the fact that my country has managed to distance itself from that problem, for we've had our share of idiots in the past. Their mindless excesses in the streets of London, as well as at Wembley, were an affront to both the people of that city and the decent Scotland supporters who travelled there. Glasgow never suffered anything like the same degree of disruption when England played at Hampden, simply because their fans never travelled there in such large numbers. I wish we had played as well as we were supported in my international matches at Wembley. We would have done a lot better.

There was no trouble when Scotland and England met in their home and away play-offs for a place in Euro 2000, but I don't think that proves anything. In fact, I would be disappointed if what happened in Belgium has not set alarm bells ringing at SFA headquarters. Scotland's football bosses have played an important role in changing the image of our national team's travelling support who are now largely self-policing. We must not become involved in any kind of situation that might undo their good work. Scotland's fans have always been good to me, and my retirement from the international scene has not changed that. I was overwhelmed by the number of get-well messages I received from them in the wake of my Tennents Scottish Cup final injury. The cards, letters, phone calls, faxes and e-mails that flooded into Pittodrie after I was stretchered off at Hampden were not just from Aberdeen supporters, they came from all over the country. I've always made a point of replying to letters from fans, but I had to make an exception in this case. You'll understand why when I tell you that Aberdeen's office staff stopped counting those messages, which filled several sacks, when they topped the 1,000 mark. I would have had another problem – writer's cramp – if I tried responding to that lot.

Seriously, I welcome this opportunity to thank everyone, including a few Manchester United fans, for taking the trouble to wish me a speedy recovery. I was touched and those messages put a smile on my sore face.

ELEVEN

My Bosses

Watching a football manager blow his top can be an unnerving experience, especially if you find yourself being singled out as a target for his wrath, but the only one of my gaffers who really frightened me was Scotland boss Jock Stein. A rollicking from the 'Big Man' was the stuff of which master-classes are made. One of his famous hard looks could, without a word being spoken, reduce your legs to jelly. But when he raised that unmistakable voice of his to spell out your shortcomings, you felt a pressing need to take a pill and lie down in a darkened room.

I caught my first blast from Stein during Scotland's preparations for the World Cup finals in Spain in 1982. It happened in the Algarve, and I can assure you that I am not likely to forget how it felt. Bounce games had been arranged against local Portuguese opposition and I came on in one of them after the interval. My first chance to touch the ball arrived via a pass-back and I anticipated no bother in gathering it, as goalkeepers were then allowed to do. The pitch was a poor one, however, and when the ball struck a divot two or three yards in front of me, I was suddenly in trouble, for it then hit my shoulder and finished up in the net. Stein went absolutely incandescent and actually came on the pitch to deliver his verdict on *my* mistake. He slaughtered me as he stood in the six–yard box and curtly dismissed my explanation about the divot. I was left cringing in embarrassment, for everyone – including some Scottish football writers – heard Stein's tirade. All I could do was wait until he ran out of a seemingly endless supply of strong language, and that seemed to take an eternity. Despite being a great manager and no mean psychologist, Stein was one of the last of the old-style managers who ruled with an iron fist. He was able to inspire more fear at club level than he did as Scotland's boss, but was never anything less than a formidable figure. I also know, for sure, that he could not half make people play for him.

Stein was one of 14 managers I served under in both club and international football. That is a sizeable number, and I think it qualifies me to speak with authority about their virtues and failings. Much though I have admired many of my gaffers, including Stein, I have to give Sir Alex Ferguson my vote as being the best of the bunch. That may surprise you in view of the wounding experience I suffered with Manchester United, but I would never let personal prejudice prevent me from telling the truth. Working with Ferguson on a day-to-day basis did not enable me to gauge the mood in which I might find him. I also regarded him as being something of a bully. But the bottom line is that, like him or not, the man is positively brilliant at his job. He may have mellowed by now, but Ferguson's rages while I worked under him at Pittodrie and Old Trafford were also impressive. I found him less scary than Stein, but extremely volatile.

I remember, in particular, the tongue-lashing he gave Aberdeen's players during the second leg of a UEFA Cup tie against Arges Pitesti in Romania in 1981.

We had won 3–0 at Pittodrie, but things went pear-shaped during the first half of the away leg when we lost two goals from dead-ball situations. That put us only one ahead and Ferguson went bananas during the half-time break. Cups flew and tea splashed across the dressing-room floor as our manager told his audience what he thought of us. He also made it very clear that we were heading for bigger trouble if we did not get our act together in the second half. We did, for we scored twice to earn a 2–2 draw and a 5–2 win on aggregate. It saved us – and the Romanian club's crockery – from further punishment. Newspapers loved it when Ferguson's anger surfaced in public, but I know he hated the 'Furious Fergie' headlines his wrath inspired.

It was Ally MacLeod, whose name will forever be linked with the World Cup finals in Argentina in 1978, who signed me for Aberdeen. He had left to become our national team's boss before I was called up to Pittodrie, so it would be unfair of me to assess his qualities as a club manager. What I do know, of course, is that his bubbling enthusiasm was infectious. How else could he have convinced an entire country that his squad could strike gold in Argentina? Despite the brevity of our association, it was MacLeod who gave me my first taste of foreign action. I was a provisional signing at the time, still playing for my Junior club, Dalry Thistle, and working as a civil servant, when he phoned my home at two o'clock in the morning. My mother woke me up to tell me that Aberdeen's manager was on the line and I was still half asleep when I took the call. What MacLeod had to say soon concentrated my mind, for he quickly explained that Aberdeen, who were about to make an end-of-season trip to Yugoslavia, had a goalkeeping crisis. Bobby Clark was already injured and Ally McLean had broken his finger playing for the reserves. MacLeod wanted to know if I could get time off work to make the trip, but it was more of a summons than a request. It was also the kind of opportunity I could not afford to miss and that was how I came to make a totally unexpected debut – against Kikinda – on foreign soil.

It was during that trip, in May 1977, that MacLeod told Aberdeen's players he was taking on the Scotland job. I could hardly believe that Dalry Thistle's goalkeeper was among the first to hear such dramatic news. I later made my Scotland debut at Under-21 level under MacLeod.

Incidentally, my poor running earned me a nickname – 'Brendan Foster' – when I went up to Pittodrie for two weeks' trial. I always finished last as we galloped up and down sand dunes, but learned a few tricks in so doing. Making yourself invisible was one of them, and it was Joe Harper, the former Scotland striker, who taught me how that was done. By the time I staggered back to the bus after one of our most gruelling sessions, I found Joe, who had obviously decided enough was enough, lying fast asleep on the back seat.

Billy McNeill had taken over from MacLeod when I was called up by Aberdeen, and I was promptly farmed out to Highland League club Deveronvale. Despite that, McNeill made me feel very much a part of the Pittodrie scene and showed great interest in my progress. Every Monday morning he wanted to know how I played for Deveronvale on the Saturday. I can I assure you that they were comprehensive interviews. He also got me good digs and handled that job personally, which was something I appreciated. I could not have had a worse start to my season with Deveronvale, for after 13 games we had only one point. My goal was being bombarded every week and I felt so sorry for myself that I asked McNeill to take me *out* of the firing line. My request was refused. 'Hang in there,' said McNeill. 'You are learning a lot from these games and that it what is important.' It was sound advice. Deveronvale's fortunes eventually changed and a season that had started so badly became a good one for them and me. We also won a cup for the first time in years. I finished up enjoying myself, and it was all thanks to McNeill's words of wisdom. I rate his style of management very highly indeed.

Ferguson, who had made a name for himself with St Mirren was my next manager, taking over after McNeill moved to Celtic. The trophies we won under his stewardship speak for themselves, but so does the manner in which he broke the Old Firm's domination of Scottish football. That was no easy trick, but it was achieved in style. It was under Ferguson that I made my Premier Division debut in 1978. Bobby Clark, our first-choice goalkeeper, had dislocated his thumb in a pre-season friendly against Tottenham at Pittodrie, and I was given the chance to show what I could do in the first 45 minutes of another friendly against Middlesbrough two days later. I must have put up a reasonable show, for I was selected for our opening League match against Hearts at Tynecastle on the Saturday and my debut was marked with a victory. Despite losing an early goal, we won 4–1. I was an experienced international by the time Ferguson left for Manchester United in 1986 and was replaced by Ian Porterfield. The new boss was an unbelievably nice guy and, after the bully-boy style of Ferguson, it was like moving from one extreme to another.

To be blunt, Porterfield was too nice for his own good. People took advantage of him. He was fortunate in that he had good professionals to work with, players who were too disciplined to step out of line, but our supporters did not take to him. I remember a very funny affair involving Porterfield after he had decided that a change of tactics was in order for a game against Rangers at Ibrox. Their strikers, Ally McCoist and Robert Fleck, had made life difficult for us on a previous occasion, and our manager told us that he had drawn up his plans accordingly. He told us what he wanted in the pre-match team-talk but our captain, Willie Miller, was clearly unimpressed by what he had heard and did not hesitate to impart that view to the rest of us. 'Forget all that,' said Willie afterwards. 'We'll play as we normally do.' We did as our captain instructed and Miller, would you believe, scored the only goal of the game. But that did not stop Porterfield speaking about his change of tactics at the after-match press conference. The last thing Porterfield did at Pittodrie was selling me to Manchester United. He was sacked the week after I left for England. In fairness, however, following in Ferguson's footsteps had been an extremely difficult task.

My time with Ferguson at Old Trafford is well documented elsewhere in this book, so is my service under Stainrod at Dundee. I did not care for the 'Wimbledon' style of play favoured by Stainrod, but I'll give him credit for being man enough to tell me he did not like me to my face. At least that let me know where I stood. Ferguson is the bench-mark for all the club managers I've had, so who comes closest to him? It may surprise you to know that Alex Miller, who took me to Hibs, gets the vote.

Miller is the antithesis of the flamboyant team boss who likes nothing better than the sound of his own voice, but he knows the game inside out. He can read play far better than many managers with much bigger reputations, and his training methods are excellent. It is fair to say that Miller's quiet, understated style has not helped him in terms of his media image, but that does not detract from my admiration for him. He also remains a good friend and someone I would not hesitate to turn to for advice. I think Miller was too loyal to Hibs. I also believe that he stayed too long at Easter Road, where he was often obliged to work on a shoestring. I am sure he must have turned down offers from elsewhere during his service with the Edinburgh club, which was ended by his resignation. I've spoken of my regard for Jocky Scott, who spent two months in the role of caretaker boss following Miller's departure, so that brings me to Jim Duffy. Like Stainrod, Duffy seemed to favour the long-ball game and I thought him a limited manager. As he made it clear that he was not interested in keeping me at Easter Road, I was able to rejoin Aberdeen with a clear conscience.

My next gaffer, Roy Aitken, was someone I really liked. We had been Scotland team-mates and I enjoyed many a battle with him at club level when he played for Celtic. Unfortunately, our new association as manager and player did not last long. Aitken was sacked after a 5-0 defeat by Dundee United at Tannadice in November. While I felt for him, his dismissal was no surprise. Aberdeen's results had been poor prior to his dismissal. Alex Miller and I were reunited at Pittodrie after that, and I was deeply involved in the moves that led to him quitting his job as assistant to Coventry boss Gordon Strachan and returning to Scotland. I spoke at length to both Aberdeen chairman Stewart Milne and director Keith Burkinshaw about Miller's qualities and 'sold' the Pittodrie post to Alex. Miller came but could not conquer. He was dismissed just over a year later and I felt bad about having persuaded him to take the job in the first place.

Paul Hegarty, Miller's former assistant, stepped into the breach as caretaker boss, and although he dropped me that season, I would not say a word against him. Paul is as honest as the day is long and was doing what he thought best for Aberdeen when he left me out of his team. You can't argue with that even if you think it was the wrong decision. Hegarty stayed in charge until the end of the 1998–99 season. Aberdeen then announced that Danish coach Ebbe Skovdahl, my current boss, would be their new manager. Skovdahl, who came from Brondby, is my first foreign boss. He also has the most laid-back attitude to life, as well as football, that I've ever encountered. At first, he thought I was too old to play for Aberdeen, so I had to work hard on making him change his mind.

Andy Roxburgh was my third boss at full international level – following Stein and Ferguson – and the fact that we still exchange Christmas cards is an indication of how well we got on together. Having said that, Roxburgh made a few mistakes at the start of his reign. Kenny Dalglish was one of his heroes and it showed. He seemed to be in awe of Kenny and treated him with far too much respect. He also tended to treat us like schoolboys. Perhaps that was a consequence of his teaching background and the fact that his previous involvement with international teams had been at a younger level, but what I can tell you, with certainty, is that it did not go down too well with the more experienced hands in Scotland's squad. Roxburgh, a meticulous planner, was smart enough to learn from such mistakes as he grew into the job. For example, team-talks that had sometimes lasted an hour were cut to 20 minutes! I found him an excellent talker on the game and was greatly impressed by his attention to detail. He could tell us everything about our opponents and their style of play. I suspect he also knew what they were having for their pre-match meal. Roxburgh did a good job for Scotland in circumstances that became increasingly difficult.

Craig Brown, Roxburgh's successor, is another boss who pays a great deal of attention to detail. As Roxburgh's assistant, he saw his boss's early mistakes at close quarters and, as a result, has been able to avoid repeating them. Brown makes sure that everything humanly possible is done for the benefit of his players. I know, from personal experience, that they are extremely well looked after. I also know how hard he has worked on building up a terrific team spirit within his squads. He has been extremely successful in that respect, for the feeling of togetherness he has created is possibly as near as you can hope to get to a club-style atmosphere. Brown's unfailing loyalty to his players is responsible for that state of affairs. He continues to involve them in the Scotland scene, even if they have temporarily fallen out of favour with their clubs. Players respond to that kind of treatment. They want to repay his loyalty. Even if they know they will not be in the team, they give him 100 per cent in training and their willingness to please helps his preparations no end.

I started this chapter with a Stein story, so I'll finish with another.

The memory of it still makes me smile, but I can think of no better illustration of Stein's wizardry in terms of man-management. Scotland's squad was staying at the Marine Hotel in Troon, and I was sharing a room with goalkeeping colleague Billy Thomson. We both felt peckish one night and, as it was after ten o'clock, decided to ring room service. We ordered a pot of tea and some sandwiches and, shortly afterwards, there was a knock at the door. I opened it and discovered, much to my surprise, that the waiter was Stein. Not a word was spoken as he set down the tray and left the room, but we were left with an uneasy feeling that all was not well. We trained at Kilmarnock's Rugby Park the following day and again the manager said nothing. But when that session was over, Stein told us to stay behind. He then took us for extra training himself and proceeded to unleash a barrage of shots at us. So hard did he work us that we were on the point of being physically sick when he finally called a halt. We staggered to the team coach that day and, as we boarded, heard Stein's voice booming out from the front seat. He was speaking to his assistant, Jim McLean, but he obviously intended being heard by everyone. 'Jim, did you ever see that *Midnight Sandwich Eaters* film?' he asked. 'No, I didn't, Jock,' replied McLean. 'Well, here come the two stars now,' said Stein.

The manager never made another reference to what had happened the previous evening, but we got the message. Late-night room service was not on the Scotland squad's agenda.

TWELVE

A Magnificent Seven (and Others)

Aberdeen can count themselves lucky if they unearth another player as good as Willie Miller this century – and I would not bet on them enjoying such good fortune. That is how highly I rate my former club captain and international team-mate. Miller was the granite rock on which was built the most successful period in Aberdeen's history. He was also the finest penalty box defender I have ever seen. I make no apology for there being five Pittodrie men in my 'magnificent seven' because all of them were special players. None more so than Miller, who led by example and was as brave as a lion. I never saw him shirk a tackle, even when he knew his challenge would almost certainly result in him being hurt. Nor did he lose many. So well did Willie perfect his role as a sweeper that he frequently got me out of jail after I had made mistakes, but I was not the only one who enjoyed his protection. He seemed to materialise, as if by magic, when any of our other defenders required his assistance. As an Aberdeen rookie, I had to work hard to gain Willie's confidence and approval. He had been accustomed to playing in front of Bobby Clark, the excellent and very experienced goalkeeper I succeeded at Pittodrie, and he was not prepared to accept anything less than Clark's standards from me. It took me a year to reach the level of consistency he expected from me, and even then I was never allowed to rest on my laurels. If I made a mistake, I would be treated to one of the famous Miller stares which threatened to burn a hole in my jersey. Don't get me wrong, Willie was a non-stop moaner who could make your ears ring. His stares were, however, in a class of their own.

Willie, only 20 when he was made Aberdeen's captain, could never claim to be one of the fastest defenders in the business. In fact it was usually yours truly who saved him from the ignominy of finishing last in our training runs. Having said that there is no doubt that his brain worked quicker than most. He wasn't tall, but his reading of play was uncanny and his wonderful timing enabled him to beat many a bigger opponent in the air. That same timing took him to where his presence was most needed as if by radar. Willie made an art form of kicking people fairly. I know that sounds like a contradiction, but it isn't. I wish I had a pound for every time I saw him take both ball and man in his superbly timed interventions. It was also claimed (by supporters of other Scottish clubs) that he refereed games as well, but that was a charge he always vehemently denied! Willie was not a morning person. It usually took him until midday to feel like having a conversation. I learned that the hard way when I shared a room with him on international trips. I had to be as quiet as a mouse until he was ready to get out of bed and woe betide me if I switched on the TV. He seemed to sleep for most of the day on such trips. Napping was his favourite way of spending any of the Scotland squad's spare time, but it's not a bad idea. I know a lot of top players who take every opportunity to rest as a means of conserving energy. Willie had opportunities to move from Aberdeen, but was happy at Pittodrie and saw no need to leave. I know he has no regrets about turning down offers from Sunderland and Rangers and I'm grateful that he did. Without him, I would not have won a fraction of the medals I've collected. I was not the only one to profit from Miller's loyalty to Aberdeen. He also helped Alex McLeish to settle in as his partner in the heart of our defence. Willie was the bolt that clamped together the Miller–McLeish–Leighton partnership that became known as 'The Triangle.' That piece of geometry served Scotland well, too, for the records show that Miller earned 65 caps and McLeish 77. Along with my 91 caps that is a grand total of 233. It has been my experience that the really good players have an average level of performance that they never drop beneath. In Willie's case, his average was higher than many other people's best. Enough said about this warrior, otherwise he'll begin to think I like him!

As you have probably guessed, McLeish is the next Don on my list and I think I am particularly well qualified to talk about a player whose successful move into management does not surprise me. We both come from Renfrewshire and I played with and against him while we were at school – Alex in Barrhead and me in Johnstone. We were also Glasgow United team-mates, and even travelled up on the train together when Aberdeen summoned us for trials. While I sprouted in my late teens, Alex was always tall and did not need his red hair to make him stand out. A commanding centre-half, he never looked anything other than a safe bet to reach the top in the professional game. Like the rest of the great Scots on my list, McLeish was a courageous player. He never opted out of his responsibilities and positively relished taking on Rangers and Celtic – especially in Glasgow. I've already described the equaliser for us against Rangers in the 1982 Scottish Cup final at Hampden. As Alex developed, he became an all-round player. As well as contributing goals, he could make good use of the ball and was able to instigate attacks. What impressed me most, however, was his burning desire to win – even in training games. It was not by chance that Alex,

Willie and I formed what some people regarded as an almost telepathic understanding in Aberdeen's defence. We worked hard on minimising our mistakes as a unit. Win or lose, the three of us would hold our own after-match post-mortems and analyse situations in which we thought we might have done better. We might not have been, as some observers suggested, joined at the hip, but we did put our heads together on a regular basis!

Doug Rougvie, another defender I was always glad to have in front of me, was a huge favourite at Pittodrie. The sight of this powerfully built player surging upfield was enough to put our support in a lather. Doug, who had a great physique, enjoyed provoking a reaction from the crowd no matter where Aberdeen were playing. At Celtic Park, he would deliberately detach himself from the rest of us to do his pre-match warm-up right in front of the 'Jungle', and he went through the same routine at Ibrox. The bold Rougvie never turned a hair when he was subjected to a torrent of abuse from the home fans in close proximity to him. In fact, he wound them up even more by responding with a gap-toothed grin. Doug's robust style and air of menace earned him a lot of criticism away from Pittodrie. It is also true to say that he succeeded in putting the fear of death into some wingers. I know for a fact that Celtic's Davie Provan did not relish having this big fellow breathing down his neck. The funny thing is that, behind Rougvie's scary image, was a really nice guy who, when not on the pitch, would not have hurt a fly. Fifer Doug earned his unusual nickname – 'The Ballingry Bat' – as a consequence of his willingness to fly through the air in an impressive dive if a winger was brave enough to make contact with one of his long legs. He was the butt of many a dressing-room leg-pull, usually instigated by Gordon Strachan. But to his credit, he never took offence.

Big Doug laughed his way through life, but he was a real gladiator of a player and a great man to have in your side. It was a sad day for all of us, team-mates and fans, when he left Pittodrie to try his luck in England. He was greatly missed.

Joker Strachan, a little man with a fantastic engine, comes next. There was never a dull moment with Gordon around, but beneath that razor-sharp wit was a dedicated professional and a world-class midfielder. Gordon was often too brave for his own good. When defenders sent him sprawling on the deck with hefty tackles, he bounced up again like a rubber ball and got on with the game. I am sure he would have earned more penalties for us if, like some of today's players, he had stayed down, feigning injury. Gordon's courage also manifested itself when he was having a bad game. He never hid or stopped calling for the ball. We loved him for that, even when he was getting pelters from our fans. Foreign clubs knew all about Gordon's ability to finish as well as create and he was invariably man-marked in European ties. His answer to that ploy was to drift all over the field, turning up in a striking role or even at left-back.

So hard did our mighty atom work those markers that, after an hour of chasing him all over the place, their legs had turned to rubber and their tongues were hanging out. Gordon would then slip back into his usual position and proceed to wreak havoc on our opponents in what seemed like overdrive. The same thing often happened in domestic encounters. It was thanks to Gordon's gradual destruction of his marker that we won many a game in the last 30 minutes. Gordon did everything in his power to help me settle in when I joined him at Old Trafford, and I think Coventry are fortunate to have him as their manager. The certainty is that his players won't be able to pull the wool over his eyes.

Neil Simpson was a ball-winning midfielder and a very different type from Strachan, but still my kind of player. He had a heart the size of a house and used his considerable strength to the full. 'Simmie' could not give a toss about an opponent's reputation. It was all the same to him if he was facing a big-name foreign player or a part-timer with a club in the lower reaches of the game. He proved that when he came on as a half-time substitute when Scotland played France in Marseilles in June 1984, for the first thing he did was put French superstar Michel Platini up in the air. Platini, who tasted European Championship glory in his team's victory over Spain in the Paris final later that month, must have been impressed by Neil's enthusiasm. He certainly wasn't upset, for he was happy to exchange shirts with the Scot after France's 2–0 victory.

'Simmie' was so proud of that shirt that he insisted on taking it to bed with him that night. There was no way he was going to risk having it pinched or go missing from his luggage at the airport. It is sad that Neil will probably be best remembered for the Pittodrie tackle which inflicted a career-threatening injury on Rangers's Ian Durrant. I'd left Aberdeen by then and have no intention of expressing an opinion on the circumstances in which Durrant was hurt. What I will say, however, is that my former team-mate was not a dirty player. Neil received a lot of hate mail in the wake of Durrant's injury and, being a sensitive type of person, the affair scarred him mentally. He was never the same player after that.

Now that I've dealt with five dandy Dons, I'll move on to Kenny Dalglish. If he had a flaw in his playing make-up, it never revealed itself to me. He was the complete footballer – strong, quick and immensely talented. Like Willie Miller, his brain worked overtime to keep him at least one move ahead of the less perceptive. Kenny scored all kinds of goals, from wonder shots to simple tap-ins, and created more than his fair share of chances for others. I'm sure Ian Rush's strike rate for Liverpool would not have been so high without the opportunities Dalglish manufactured for him on a regular basis. I can't come to terms with the fact that Kenny's managerial image is one of dourness because he was great fun to be with as a player. I've seen him take over the whole dining room on Scotland trips and have us in stitches. Perhaps he found a lot more to laugh at when he had only his own game to worry about. I've seen how the stress of bossing a team can change someone's personality. It is not a role I hanker after. I'd much rather stick to coaching.

Graeme Souness, a cocky, arrogant Scot with bags of style, would be in any team of world-class players I was given the chance to select. Nobody scared this man, for the simple reason that he couldn't half look after himself. He also gave the impression that you would probably hurt yourself trying to kick him. Graeme's powerful legs and massive thighs discouraged opponents from harbouring any thoughts of taking liberties with him, but he was also an elegant midfielder and a master of the defence-splitting pass. His accuracy with the ball was a joy to watch and I think it is significant that he was a success in Italy, where the standard of top club football is extremely high. I'll never forget Graeme's pre-match battle order to Liverpool's players as they stood in the tunnel before the first leg of their European Cup tie at Pittodrie. 'Come on, chaps, let's get into these Jocks,' he said crisply. That was it. Our challenge had been dismissed in one short, sharp sentence and we were left gob-smacked. At the same time, I could not help but admire a player with such huge self-confidence. Graeme believed he was a superstar – and indeed he was!

What about the best foreign players I've faced? I've drawn up a list of six and, not surprisingly, it contains two Brazilians – Rivaldo and Ronaldo. Rivaldo has two fantastic feet and thoroughly deserves to be rated one of the best players in the world. But what caught my eye when I faced him in the World Cup in France was his capacity for hard work. Unlike some big-name players who wait until they are in possession of the ball before showing what they can do, Rivaldo is quite happy to track back and help out team-mates. He has that great knack of always making himself available to receive the ball. Rivaldo's shooting power is also breath-taking. He unleashed a cracker at my goal in Paris and I was delighted to see it whip past the post. I could not have done anything to stop that effort if it had been on target.

Ronaldo's pace off a standing start is frightening. He runs faster with the ball than some players can without it. I thought we handled him well in Paris, but there was an air of expectancy in the stadium every time he was in possession. We all know that, because of his problems, Ronaldo should never have played in the final of France '98, but I'll go along with Rivaldo who says that, if fit, his Brazilian colleague is the best in the business.

Platini, the gifted Frenchman who was on the receiving end of that Simpson challenge in Marseilles, is another of my foreign favourites. I've never seen anyone able to combine the roles of midfield creator and striker as well as he did. He could sniff out scoring opportunities before they had developed and his wonderful partnership alongside Jean Tigana and Alain Giresse was something very special. It was the platform on which France built an excellent team.

Franz Beckenbauer, the German midfield ace who stepped back to become an equally big success as a sweeper, is probably the most graceful defender I'll see in my lifetime. It did not seem to matter to him if he was closely marked, for he could always find time to control the ball and make excellent use of it. He read the game brilliantly and delivered passes of stunning accuracy over any distance. A delicate chip or a raking crossfield ball perfectly timed to catch a player in full flight, Beckenbauer made it all look so simple during a brilliant career which earned him a glittering pile of medals and 103 caps. He also enjoyed the distinction of winning the World Cup as both a captain and a manager. Beckenbauer had class written all over him and it went beyond his talent on the pitch.

I recall him standing out in the snow to be interviewed for British TV after helping Hamburg knock Aberdeen out of the UEFA Cup in Germany in 1981. Asked about his fee, 'Kaiser Franz' told the interviewer to donate the money to a charity of his own choice.

You may find this hard to believe, but the best striker of a ball I've had to face was another sweeper – Bayern Munich's Klaus Augenthaler. This player needed no encouragement to let fly and his shots were like guided missiles. Every time Augenthaler advanced into Aberdeen's half in our Cup-Winners' Cup clash with Bayern in Germany, he was looking to have a pop at my goal from anything up to 40 yards out. When his drive beat me in the return leg at Pittodrie, it was from 20 yards and with no backlift.

Little did I know when I played against Franco Baresi in an Under-21 international that he would go on to become one of the legends of Italian football. Baresi was not a big man, but he ran his country's defence, and that of AC Milan, with authority and efficiency. Quick in thought as well as deed, Baresi was the padlock on his rearguard's door and his interpretation of the sweeper's role made him one of the most influential figures in world football. Such players are extremely difficult, perhaps even impossible, to replace. I felt sorry for Baresi when he missed from the spot in Italy's penalty shoot-out with Brazil in the World Cup final in Los Angeles in 1994, for he was one of the main reasons why that game finished in a no-scoring draw after extra time.

As a postscript to my thoughts on a few of the foreign stars I've played against, I must say that, like every other Scot, I was dazzled by the quality of play we saw in Euro 2000. It was, as they say, as good as it gets. The down side is, of course, that master craftsmen like Zinedine Zidane and Luis Figo unwittingly conspired to give our domestic game an impossible act to follow – especially since a new season came so quickly after they had quit their summer stage. That may be no bad thing, however, if it affects the thinking of some of our club managers and coaches in a positive way. I've no doubt the vast majority of supporters would back any efforts to produce more artistry and, as a consequence, less mediocrity. Scottish football fans loved watching the skills that were paraded in Belgium and Holland. They are not daft enough to expect the same level of creativity on their own doorstep, but there is no doubt that they would appreciate a hint of better things to come.

THIRTEEN

People and Places

I don't think there is any doubt that the Japanese will make a superb job of co-hosting the 2002 World Cup with South Korea. Having visited Japan with both Manchester United and Scotland, I am convinced that this country's contribution to the staging of the next finals will be something special. I'm also betting that, regardless of what are likely to be sky-high prices, the football crazy Japanese will snap up every ticket they can lay hands on, thus ensuring that all the games played within their territory will be complete sell-outs. Japan, where cash has been ploughed into the building of magnificent stadiums, is by far the most expensive place to which my travels have taken me. If Scotland qualify for the 2002 finals, it will cost the tartan army an arm and a leg to follow them there. As well as facing hefty bills for flights and hotels, they will have to budget for paying mind-boggling prices for meals and drinks. In such circumstances, it will be no problem for them to stay both slim and sober. Having said that, there is no way I want Scotland's team and the more adventurous of their followers to miss out on an historic event.

It was a huge disappointment when our national squad failed to make it to the US for that country's début as World Cup hosts, and I would not like to see the Scots again marked absent at another first in the Far East.

I had the honour of captaining my country in Japan when we played them and Ecuador there in the Kirin Cup, a triangular tournament, in May, 1995. The SFA were fiercely criticised for agreeing to take players on such a long journey at that time of year and there was a glut of call-offs from Craig Brown's squad, but perhaps it was not such a bad idea as many people then thought. If we do earn a place in the 2002 finals, the fact that players like Paul Lambert and Craig Burley have already seen action in Japan could be a plus mark of some significance. The knowledge gained on what was dismissed as being no more than a jaunt could also be of great assistance to team boss Brown. Lambert made his Scotland début in our no-scoring draw with Japan in Hiroshima's Big Arch Stadium. We then beat Ecuador 2–1 in Toyama, with our goals coming from John Robertson and Steve Crawford. Our patched-up squad had the satisfaction of returning home undefeated.

I found Japan a fascinating place and my earlier visit with Manchester United enabled me to gauge their rate of progress as a football nation. It's impressive, and I'm not surprised that a growing number of foreign players and coaches are being attracted to the J League clubs. As well as the adulation of the fans, they can earn a lot of money.

Japanese fans are extremely knowledgeable about the European soccer scene. They love the game and never tire of talking about it. Take it from me, if we make it to that big party in 2002, they'll make us more than welcome.

Japan is one of the 44 countries in which I've played, and I'm grateful to football for giving me the chance to see the world. The game has also opened doors which would otherwise have been closed to me. If I'd stayed in my job as a civil servant I don't think I would have been invited to dance on the stage at a packed Madison Square Gardens. That happened when Scotland's squad attended a Rod Stewart concert in the US during our build-up to Euro 96. Rock star Rod asked the players to join him on the stage for his final number, 'Twisting the Night Away', and then insisted we do just that. I was reluctant to dance in front of so many people, but took my cue from Craig Brown. The national team boss was, as they say, a good mover. Scotland fan Rod also trained with us in the US and his presence in our ranks attracted a bigger crowd than you will see at some of our First Division matches. The Rangers players in our squad were none too pleased when Rod appeared wearing a Celtic jersey, but Craig Brown knows a thing or two about diplomacy. He saved our guest from the distinct possibility of taking a few hard knocks by handing him a national team top.

Sticking with the showbiz theme, I've also been involved in the making of seven records with Scotland, Aberdeen and Manchester United. Despite the fact that I can't sing a note, I've made noises alongside the likes of Rod, Fish, Donnie Munro and B.A. Robertson. It's fair to say I'm not my family's favourite vocalist, either. In fact, when I burst into song at home my daughter and son can be counted on to give me a hard time. My unfailing reply is that, unlike my two critics, I've had the distinction of appearing on *Top of the Pops*. I've also made a couple of appearances on another TV show – *A Question of Sport* – as both a panellist and mystery guest.

My most embarrassing moment abroad was during a trip to Egypt with Aberdeen. There was the usual exchange of club emblems before we played a game in Ismailia and our players were already heading back from the centre circle when I spotted the Egyptian goalkeeper running towards me holding a pennant. I decided to meet him halfway, but soon wished I had not bothered. Along with the pennant, he gave me a big wet kiss on the lips. My

IN THE FIRING LINE

Aberdeen team-mates were convulsed with laughter as I made a red-faced retreat to my goal and my discomfort did not end there. To my dismay, I found myself sitting opposite the kissing keeper at the after-match meal. Every time I looked up from my plate, I found him nodding and smiling at me. I don't scare easily, but I'll admit to being in a state of fear and alarm during that meal. So much so that I did not dare leave my seat to go to the toilet.

I had another unnerving experience during a meal on the banks of the Nile when a large insect crawled out of an ashet on our table. A straight-faced Eric Black summoned a waiter, showed him the creepy-crawly and said that I'd ordered my food well done. Needless to say, none of the players felt like eating after that. All this was nothing compared to the fright some of our players were given on a visit to the Sphinx and Pyramids. Having had their fill of sightseeing, they decided to try a camel ride. It seemed a harmless bit of fun, but it did not turn out that way. After being led to a quiet spot, the camel drivers then drew knives and demanded money from them. There is no doubt that it was a scary incident, but I think those Egyptians should have known better than ask men from Aberdeen for cash.

Estonia has a special place among my memories of foreign trips and it should not be difficult to guess why. It was, of course, the scene of what is rightly regarded as one of the most amazing affairs in the history of international football – the World Cup qualifying tie that never was. I'll never forget the sight of Scotland's team starting a match in which the opposition was nowhere to be seen. Sub-standard floodlights at the Tallinn ground had led to the tie's kick-off time being brought forward, but Estonia's team didn't turn up. I still don't understand why they were not immediately chucked out of the competition.

That was not the only non-event I've been involved in, either. When Aberdeen went to Albania for a European Cup-Winners' Cup tie against Dinamo Tirana, the news back home was that we had been caught up in an attempted military coup. The truth of the matter is that we were in no danger whatsoever. A handful of armed men had attempted to land on one of the country's beaches, but they had been shot or captured. On top of that, the incident occurred before our arrival in Tirana. It was because of Albania's self-imposed isolation and the lack of communication between that country and the rest of Europe that the story grew wings. The citizens of Tirana were so unused to seeing visitors from the west that they could not stop staring at us. In turn, we could not get over the sight of women carrying hods full of bricks. I'll remember Albania as a land of cyclists and pedestrians. I was told cars were in such short supply that couples had to make an official application to have one take them to their wedding.

One of the fiercest foreign encounters I've been involved in was with Aberdeen in Neuchâtel, Switzerland, and it was supposed to be a friendly. We thought we were to play a Swiss select, but found ourselves facing what was virtually the full national team. Significantly, the opposition included two Swiss stars, Egli and Hermann, who felt they had a score to settle with our captain. Both had suffered a broken nose as a consequence of clashing with Willie Miller in an international, and it was clear that they were seeking revenge. They glared at him before the match and made signs to indicate that it was now their turn to inflict damage on Willie's nose. How our skipper escaped injury I'll never know, for he was the prime target for some of the wildest punches I've seen thrown outside a boxing ring. The Swiss did not neglect the rest of us, either, so that so-called friendly became a battle in which the ball was frequently an irrelevance. Boots and fists flew as blows were traded all over the field, and it was 90 minutes of absolute mayhem. It's fair to say that, despite being beaten 1-0, we gave our opponents as good as we got. We also considered ourselves fortunate to avoid serious casualties. The Swiss may be a peace-loving nation, but that punch-up in Neuchatel proved that they know how to go to war on a football pitch.

Aberdeen was involved in another pre-season battle in West Germany, and again it came out of the blue. We were taking part in a tournament hosted by a club from one of that country's lower leagues and did not expect trouble in our opening game against them. What we did not know, however, was that the local team's coach was intent on ruffling our manager's feathers. There had been bad blood between the two men as players, and it soon became clear that he wanted the satisfaction of giving Alex Ferguson's men a hard time. That lit the fuse for a ferocious kicking match, which did nothing for Anglo-German relations. Neither did a cry from Neil Simpson to 'get into these German Bs', for his message was perfectly understood by our opponents. We saved the tournament organiser from having a heart attack by beating the home team on penalties after a 2–2 draw. As the script had been written for Aberdeen to meet Dinamo Bucharest in the final, he was a very relieved man.

It was as a result of our lunchtime kick-off against West Germany in the World Cup finals in Mexico that I found myself in the hands of the police. Along with Paul McStay and Roy Aitken, I'd decided to go to chapel that evening, but we were told there was no way we could leave our team's hotel without being escorted. As a result, the three of us found ourselves sitting like criminals behind the wire mesh grill in the back of a police car. Reporters spotted us when we stopped at a crossing and I'm sure that, even if only for a moment, some of them must have wondered whether they had stumbled on a good story. After all, three Scotland stars arrested in Mexico is the stuff of which headlines are made. What a disappointment it must have been when these sharp-eyed scribes quickly worked out the reason for our trio being in the hands of the law.

The snag about playing at the top for as long as I've done is that it makes you an easy target for dressing-room jokes. My dress sense is under constant attack from the young players at Pittodrie. If I wear a suit, I'm asked if I had it at the 1974 World Cup. I took a lot of stick when Scotland's players had their bags rifled at Athens airport because mine was left intact. Darren Jackson claimed the thieves had taken pity on me because of my old-fashioned clothes.

Souvenirs remind me of the good, bad and funny times I've had in foreign parts. There is also no danger of me forgetting that the only time I was attacked by a fan was not in one of the hot spots I've landed in abroad, but in my own country. It happened during a match against Motherwell at Fir Park in the first season of my second spell with Aberdeen. After Dean Windass had scored an injury-time winner for us from the penalty spot, I noticed one of our defenders, Tony Kombouare, waving to me. What I did not realise was that it was a warning. Unknown to me, a fan had come out of the crowd and was heading in my direction. The next thing I knew, I was being knocked down by a punch on the back of the head. I got an apology from my attacker, who wrote to me from prison. He even gave me his Barlinnie cell number.

FOURTEEN

The Last Line

Every young player has at least one hero, someone he can look up to, and goalkeepers are no exception. Mine was Pat Jennings, the former Arsenal and Tottenham idol, and studying the way that great Irishman went about his business was part of my education. I've never tried to model myself on someone else because I don't think that works. We are all made differently, so copying a style that may not fit you any better than borrowed clothes does not make sense. The trick is to pick up good ideas and adapt them to suit your individual requirements. That way you will feel comfortable with any adjustments you may make to your game. You'll also stay your own man and be better equipped to accept the responsibility of working out where you have gone wrong when you are having a bad spell.

I would not want any young goalkeeper to set his sights on becoming a replica of Jim Leighton. For a start, he could never hope to have legs like mine unless he bought himself a horse. But seriously, I see no virtue in slavish imitation. There was nothing flash about Jennings, who made 119 appearances for Northern

Ireland, and that was one of the reasons why he became my hero. His style was to make a save look as basic and simple as possible, and that rubbed off on me. Like him, I've never indulged in making my job look more difficult. It may please the crowd when a goalkeeper does a spectacular forward roll after making a save, but I'd much rather concentrate my efforts on being efficient. Jennings has huge hands, a decided advantage in our line of work, and could pluck balls out of the air like a fruit-picker, but what also caught my attention was the number of important saves he made with his feet. That was a tip worth taking and I had no hesitation in putting it to good use. Developing the ability to stop shots in this way has stood me in good stead. I've lost count of the number of times one of my outstretched legs has prevented the loss of a goal.

I was in awe of Jennings and found myself tongue-tied when I finally met up with my hero. I played against him during my first spell with Aberdeen and we were introduced after the game. I remember that when we shook hands, mine seemed to disappear inside his. I think that Pat, one of the nicest guys I've met in football, realised I was star-struck. He certainly did his best to put me at ease in his company, but I still didn't manage to tell him that he had been my revered teacher.

Alan Rough, the man I succeeded in Scotland's team, was probably the most naturally gifted goalkeeper I have ever seen. Alas, he was also the laziest. Had his desire and ambition matched his ability, he could have achieved far more than he did. It could be said that the laid-back character we knew as 'Scruff' did not do too badly. After all, he earned more than 50 caps. But I honestly believe he could have made a name for himself with one of British football's biggest clubs if only he had wanted that badly enough. It was clear that he didn't, otherwise he would not have spent most of his career with Partick Thistle. I mean no disrespect to Thistle, but it would be fair to say that they are not one of our fashionable clubs and I think that Rough could have bettered himself long before he finally departed from Firhill to join Hibs. That said, I thought Alan had a great attitude in terms of coping with stress. I don't think he knew the meaning of the word, for nothing seemed to bother him. He could switch from playing in front of a modest crowd at a Thistle match to appearing before 80,000 spectators at an international – without batting an eye. In fact, having roomed with him on Scotland duty, I don't believe he even gave it a thought. Alan laughed his way through life and was able to shrug off the kind of wounding criticism that would have reduced many a player to tears. I envied him in that respect and often wished I had a skin as thick as his. It would have helped me to cope with the stick I took from English football writers during my time with Manchester United. I did not handle that as well as I might have done. Unlike Alan, I let it get to me. In fairness to myself, I should point out that none of the criticism aimed at Alan in Scottish newspapers was anything like as venomous as the stuff I had written about me on the other side of the border. A likeable rascal, Alan was great company on Scotland trips. I also admired his resilience. No matter how many times his international career was written off, he kept bouncing back.

Like the rest of us, Rough had to cope with the consequences of a widely held English view that Scottish goalkeepers are a flawed breed, capable of making horrendous mistakes. That myth grew out of some heavy defeats our national team suffered in past Wembley visits, most notably the 9–3 thrashing in 1961, and has been perpetuated by TV pundits. I thought I might have done something to stem the jokes made about us by having 23 shut-outs in my first 43 games for my country, and becoming the first Scottish goalkeeper in over 100 years to play five games in a row without losing a goal, but that was before my career went off the rails at Old Trafford. In view of the crushing disappointment I suffered there, you may be surprised to know that Les Sealey, the English goalkeeper who took my place when I was dropped for Manchester United's FA Cup final replay, is one of my favourite people.

Les, a cocky Londoner, had a fall-out at Luton before he joined United on loan and as cover. He had lost interest in keeping himself in shape and was more than a stone overweight when he moved from Kenilworth Road. As a result, he had to work hard on regaining his enthusiasm, as well as his fitness, and I'd like to think I was of some assistance to him on that score. He certainly helped me, for we gelled from the moment we met and I found him very supportive. As our friendship developed, he became a regular visitor to my home and often had meals with us. I enjoyed his company and his cheeky humour. I've told the story of how Sealey tried to give me his medal after United's replay victory over Crystal Palace, but very few people know about the close-range backing he gave me during the first game.

I don't know how he did it, but the bold Les somehow worked his way into the group of photographers behind my Wembley goal and hurled encouragement at me from there. I could hardly believe my ears when I heard that familiar Cockney voice bellowing 'Come on, big man, keep going.' That was typical of Les. So was the way he did his utmost to lift my spirits after I found myself out in the cold at Old Trafford. He cursed and swore at me when he thought I was down in the dumps, and gave me a verbal kick up the backside if I showed any sign of losing the will to cope with my situation. 'It happened to me, so I'm not going to let it happen to you,' he would say. I'll be eternally grateful to Les, who is still a good friend, for going out of his way to keep my head above water through the worst days of my career. I've also found it useful to repeat the Sealey message to other players who have been going through a bad spell.

Looking at the number of foreign goalkeepers now playing in Britain, it's hard to believe that our clubs once had serious reservations about recruiting them. While there were never any doubts about their athleticism, the perception of them was that they seemed ill-equipped to handle the physical style of our domestic game. In plain language, they did not fancy being knocked about and were likely to crack under pressure. Like so many of the insular attitudes which once closed our eyes to the way football was developing in the rest of the world, that notion has long since been kicked into touch. Indeed, a foreign goalkeeper is now the preferred option for many of our leading managers. As you would expect, I'm not too happy about any trend which can hamper the development of home-grown talent, but I think Manchester United's search for someone to fill the gap left by great Dane Peter Schmeichel's departure is a good example of the way the pendulum has swung. Significantly, that hunt once more led them abroad to sign Fabien Barthez, the star who helped France to an historic World Cup and European Championship double.

There is no doubt that Schmeichel, who replaced Sealey in United's team, is the best goalkeeper I've ever seen. Nor do I think he would disagree with my rating. Such was his massive self-belief, he was convinced he was better than anyone else playing in his position. It wasn't arrogance when he told you he had never lost a bad goal – as far as he was concerned it was an indisputable fact. While Schmeichel's confidence was one of his most valuable assets, there were many others. His 6 feet and 4 inches and 16-stone frame made him an imposing figure between the posts. He could also throw a ball further than many goalkeepers could kick it. The first time I saw one of Schmeichel's long-range throws was in a practice match. He picked up a pass-back and hurled the ball like a guided missile 20 yards inside the opposition's half. There was, I can tell you, a sharp intake of breath all over that pitch.

Schmeichel is an unorthodox goalkeeper. In fact, there are some aspects of his technique that I regard as being very poor. But who cares? In my book, he has proved he can do the most important thing, which is keeping the ball out of the net, better than anyone else.

Technique is not the be-all and end-all of our job. At the end of the day it's down to ability and we all do things against the book if we think it is in our best interests. How else do goalkeepers pull off so-called 'impossible' saves? Schmeichel moved to Portugal after helping United complete their glorious 'treble' and I cannot think of a more fitting exit line for this Scandinavian superman. I would also offer the thought that I do not envy any goalkeeper the task of following in his Old Trafford footsteps.

To those who persist in making jokes about the quality of Scotland goalkeepers, I offer the name of Andy Goram. They obviously haven't seen too much of this former Rangers and Hibs star who is now with Motherwell. Like Schmeichel, Andy can pull off amazing saves when all seems lost. He does not have the Dane's height and reach, but his technique is excellent and his years with Rangers taught him how to maintain his concentration during periods of inactivity. He had a sticky start to his career with Rangers, with supporters and the media giving him more criticism than he had previously experienced, but he went on to become an Ibrox hero. I received a lot of phone calls from Andy during his early days with Rangers, and I hope the advice I offered him proved useful. Over the years I seem to have become something of an agony aunt for other goalkeepers and I like to keep my 'clients' happy.

Andy, born in Bury but the son of a former Hibs goalkeeper, was with Oldham when he made his Scotland début in a no-scoring draw with East Germany at Hampden. He came on to replace me in the second half of what was also manager Alex Ferguson's first game in charge of the national team following the death of Jock Stein. Andy and I hit it off straight away and it was the start of a long association. He spent five years as my understudy until, following the World Cup finals in Italy, he took over as Scotland's first choice. The strange thing is that Andy and I were not often in genuine contention for that job. My long absence from the international scene, a consequence of my club career lurching into oblivion, was one of the reasons for that. Andy's injury problems and the walk-outs he staged from his country's squad were others. I must say I was very disappointed in him when he turned his back on Scotland prior to the Euro 96 qualifying tie against Greece at Hampden in 1995. At the time it was claimed he was not 'mentally attuned' for that game in which I played, but he has since admitted that he wanted to avoid injury and save himself for the second leg of Rangers' European Champions League qualifying tie against Anorthosis Famagusta. I've already told you about the anger I felt when Andy was preferred to me for the Euro 96 finals in England, but I also saw red during the build-up to that event. I could not believe it when Craig Brown asked me to limp off five minutes from the end of a preparatory match against Sweden in Stockholm so that Andy could earn a cap.

It was my 70th appearance for Scotland and my response to that request was there was no way I was going to devalue a special occasion by shamming injury. I was furious. Andy did replace me in goal near the end of that game, but I came off that pitch with my head held high and no sign of a limp. Brown apologised to me after the game. Despite that nonsense, which was certainly no fault of Andy's, I take off my goalkeeper's hat to him. Bad injuries, particularly those affecting his knees, have not prevented him from having an incredible career. How anyone can train as little as he does yet keep playing at a high standard is beyond me. Long may he continue. Regardless of our rivalry, Andy and I always remained good friends and were 100 per cent supportive of each other. We didn't pick Scotland's team, so there was no friction between us when one or the other was given the nod.

Andy's career could have come to an abrupt and tragic end before his £1 million transfer from Hibs to Rangers. He was lucky to escape being killed when marauding Spanish fans stoned the Scotland team's coach in Madrid in 1988. It happened after Scotland's no-score draw with Spain at the Bernabeu Stadium. Andy and I had been sitting on opposite sides of the coach, but he moved over to join me for a chat. Just as well, for a large piece of concrete then shattered a window and landed on the seat he had vacated. It was a very close call. We found ourselves being showered by flying glass, but that was nothing compared to the damage that would have been done if one of the missiles had struck a player or official. Spanish fans also attacked a group of Scottish journalists and TV men as they made their way back to their hotel after the match. It was not a good night to be out and about on the streets of Madrid.

By the way, only one international goalkeeper, Sweden's Thomas Ravelli, has refused to exchange jerseys with me after an international match. When I asked him about making a swap, he made it clear that he wasn't interested. 'Why would I want your jersey?' he said. I don't know if that response was because Sweden had just lost to Scotland. I do know that it left me speechless.

FIFTEEN

Hampden Horror Show

Last season's Tennents Scottish Cup final against Rangers was billed as my farewell appearance for Aberdeen. But that was a label that did not bear my endorsement. As I had not yet ruled out the possibility of continuing my playing career at Pittodrie, it seemed a bit premature. At the same time, the thought that the final might turn out to be my last competitive game for my club did not faze me. If it did transpire that I was heading for retirement to concentrate on a new role as Aberdeen's full-time goalkeeping coach, I felt I could not have chosen a better place to bow out than Hampden. After all, I had played there in four previous Scottish Cup finals and been on the winning side each time. I'd also been involved in many Scotland triumphs at this famous ground. It was because of all my fond memories of Hampden that I was determined to make the most of what seemed certain to be my last visit there as a competitor. I even promised myself that, win or lose, I would be the last Aberdeen player to leave the pitch. I wanted to linger there and take a long look at my surroundings before heading for the dressing-room.

After all my years in the game, I should have known better than to tempt fate by making that promise public. Instead of being the last man to quit the Hampden stage, I was the first – and I made my exit after only two minutes. My last glimpse of the stadium was from a horizontal position and through a mist of pain, for I was carried off on a stretcher with my jaw broken in two places. Let me set the record straight about what has been dubbed my Hampden horror show. I want to make it absolutely clear that I attach no blame whatsoever to Rangers striker Rod Wallace, whose knee crashed into my face after what was only my second touch of the ball. It happened when I went to scoop up a low ball squared to the front post by Andrei Kanchelskis. I saw Rod coming in out of the corner of my eye and reached forward quickly with the result that my head was higher than it might otherwise have been. It was purely accidental when Rod's standing leg then collided with my face and I have to say that he was quite within his rights to go for the ball. In fact, had I been in Rangers manager Dick Advocaat's shoes, I would have expected my player to make a challenge and demanded an explanation if he had failed to do so.

I was, of course, in no fit state to analyse that incident as I lay dazed on the Hampden turf. All I knew was that I was in serious trouble. There was a lot of blood coming from my mouth and the pain in my face was sending a clear message that my part in the final was over. I was also convinced that I had lost some teeth, but it turned out that the reason I could not locate them was because my jaw was so far out of alignment. I can assure you that the disappointment I felt as I was taken away from the pitch was just as hard to bear as those facial pains and I found myself weeping tears of frustration. 'It can't end like this, on a stretcher,' I moaned to Aberdeen physiotherapist John Sharp, but I already knew it had.

Although I was groggy and unaware of much that was happening in the wake of the accident, I heard later of the great kindness shown to my family by the Hampden staff. Along with my father, Linda, Claire and Greg had all hurried from their seats after I was hurt and they were given every assistance to be at my side as quickly as possible. They were also given an immediate assurance that my injury was not, as they had obviously feared, life-threatening. I had more good fortune in the two doctors who attended me after I was taken to the Victoria Infirmary. They had been watching the final on television while on call. As a result, they knew the nature of my injury and were actually on their way to my side before being summoned. I had a three-hour operation at the HCI in Clydebank the following day. Two plates were inserted in the right side of my face and another two in my chin, with 14 screws keeping them in place. Thanks to the innovative surgery employed, there was no need for my jaw to be wired up. Nor did I face the prospect of having those plates removed at a later date. They are permanent fixtures.

While being extremely grateful for the treatment I received at both hospitals, I cannot say I liked the look of myself after returning to my home in Aberdeen. It seemed to me that I bore a fair resemblance to the film portrayal of 'Elephant Man' John Merrick. My strange appearance was cause for concern because Linda and I were due to fly out for a holiday in St Lucia on the Thursday after my Hampden injury and I did not fancy being stared at for a fortnight. In fact, I was seriously considering cancelling the holiday when my features suddenly began to show a marked improvement. I decided that two weeks in the Caribbean sunshine was worth a few inquisitive glances, so we were off. Linda's bonus was that, due to the fact my jaw was not wired, she was spared the task of packing a liquidiser. I found I could eat fish without too much trouble and that became my staple diet during our stay in St Lucia. Towards the end of our holiday, I was even able to tackle some meat dishes.

Lying on the beach gave me time to reflect on what had been the most bizarre season of my entire career. I cannot think of any other way to describe a campaign in which Aberdeen finished bottom of the SPL, yet figured in two finals, the CIS Insurance Cup being the other competition in which we advanced to the last stage. I also thought of how prophetic my warning to manager Ebbe Skovdahl had been. Earlier in the season I had argued that not naming a goalkeeper among our three substitutes for Scottish Cup ties was taking a big risk. What would happen, I asked my boss, if his last line of defence was injured in the first minute and there was no specialist replacement? Skovdahl took my point but said he was prepared to take that risk. His view was that naming three outfield players as his subs gave him greater flexibility and a better chance of winning. I must emphasise that I do not in any way hold our manager responsible for the fix we found ourselves in at Hampden after my early departure. He had done what he thought was best in the circumstances. Rangers could have found themselves in exactly the same position, for they, too, had no goalkeeper among their three substitutes.

Having said that, there is absolutely no doubt that my early injury ruined the final as a spectacle and robbed it of its showpiece status. With no disrespect to Robbie Winters, the outfield player who took my place, there was not the remotest chance of us being able to compete with Rangers on anything resembling level terms after my departure. I'm not saying Rangers would never have gone on to win 4–0 if I had remained in Aberdeen's goal, but what I do know, for sure, is that Hampden's paying customers were short-changed. It was a farcical situation. Aberdeen had two goalkeepers, David Preece and Ryan Esson, sitting in the stand, but could not call on either of them. Thank goodness the number of Scottish Cup substitutes has since been increased from three to five, bringing the national knockout competition in line with the SPL. But what a pity that change came too late for Aberdeen and their supporters.

Inevitably, the daft ruling that was in operation at the time also removed some of the gloss from Rangers' success and that was another regrettable consequence of my injury. I'm sure the Ibrox club's fans would have enjoyed a great deal more satisfaction from their team's victory had Aberdeen not been so obviously disadvantaged. For the record, I did not know who had replaced me after I was stretchered off. It was not until later that I learned it was Winters. I felt sorry for him, for it must have seemed as if his worst nightmare had come true.

I don't mind admitting that I never expected to play at Hampden again after being dropped by Paul Hegarty, who was then Aberdeen's caretaker manager, following a 3–0 defeat from Dundee United in February 1999. It looked like the end of my first-team days at Pittodrie and I was given no encouragement to think otherwise when new boss Skovdahl took over in May. The signing of a new goalkeeper, David Preece from Darlington, seemed to spell out that, in Skovdahl's eyes, it was time for old Jim to be put out to grass. It might well have turned out that way but for the fact that Preece was injured in the 7–0 thrashing Aberdeen suffered at the hands of Celtic last season. He was so badly concussed that, despite playing on, he did not know the final score. That mishap opened the door for a comeback against Motherwell in October – eight months after Hegarty had dropped me – and my return coincided with Aberdeen recording their first win of the season. We beat Motherwell in an amazing game at Fir Park, where we won 6–5. It was also the first time in my career that I earned a win bonus after losing five goals! Although I kept my place, our team's League form was dreadful and points proved hard to come by. We seemed to save our best performances for the other competitions, and that was borne out by our progress to the final of the CIS Insurance Cup as well as the Tennents Scottish Cup.

I did not feature in Aberdeen's CIS Cup campaign until the

quarter-finals, but it was a good place to start. An Andy Dow goal gave us a 1–0 win over Rangers at Pittodrie after extra time. The result lifted some of the gloom which had descended on our club. It did not, however, save us from more SPL thrashings. Celtic won 6–0 at Pittodrie and Rangers handed us a 5–0 defeat at Ibrox before we returned to the cup trail. We overcame St Mirren, after a replay, in the third round of the Scottish Cup, and beat Dundee United 1–0 at Dens Park in the semi-final of the CIS Cup five days later. Our two meetings with St Mirren sparked a run of good results on all fronts. Reaching the final of the CIS Cup was another boost and the month of February was further brightened when we beat Inverness Caledonian Thistle, shock Scottish Cup conquerors of Celtic in Glasgow, after a replay. Our fifth-round Scottish Cup victory over Dundee United in March at Tannadice, where we won 1–0, should have put us in the right frame of mind for our CIS Cup final meeting with Celtic that month. We had suffered severe punishment at the hands of our Hampden rivals, but I did not see any reason to feel inferior to them. They were under considerable pressure to appease their fans, and in some disarray, so I thought we had a good chance of giving them more to worry about.

Unfortunately, too few of our players really believed in themselves and the possibility of overcoming their opponents. As a consequence, Celtic had little trouble in recording a 2–0 win. Having Norwegian defender Thomas Solberg sent for an early bath did not help our cause, but I offer no excuses for our defeat. The plain truth is that we did not do ourselves justice and got what we deserved.

My next visit to the national stadium was for our Scottish Cup semi-final against Hibs, my former club, and this time there was a happy outcome. We fought back, after going a goal behind, to win 2–1 with our goals coming from Arild Stavrum and Andy Dow. I could hardly believe my change of luck. Despite having written off my chances of ever returning to Hampden as a player, I was now in line to make my third appearance there in the space of only ten weeks! Our semi-final victory over Hibs was of special significance because of the fact that we would meet Rangers in the final. As the Ibrox club had already done enough to retain their Bank of Scotland SPL championship title, this meant that, regardless of how we fared against them, we were guaranteed a place in the UEFA Cup. Nice one, Dons. As I have said, last season was a roller-coaster ride for Aberdeen, full of unexpected twists and turns. But I did not enjoy having to pick the ball out of my net more times than I care to remember. It was certainly not the kind of scenario I had envisaged for my testimonial year. Our club also earned the unwanted distinction of making the worst start in its history and I don't think that our cup runs were in any way a suitable compensation for the way we staggered through our League programme. As a survivor from Aberdeen's golden era, I had to grit my teeth when, as a result of that dreadful start, we were rated the worst team in Europe. Hopefully we will never again have to suffer such an indignity.

It was on a pre-season trip to Hanover that Skovdahl first sat down with me to discuss my future. He made it pretty clear then that, as far as he was concerned, I would not be in contention for the top goalkeeping job. His view was that, at 41, I was too old for first-team duty unless in an emergency. Naturally, I did not agree with him. I felt I should be judged on merit rather than age. I also said that if I did get the chance to return to the first team, I would prove myself good enough to stay there. It wasn't an idle boast, for I was confident I could still play at the highest level. As a consequence of being involved in the World Cup finals in France, I had been tired and jaded when Hegarty dropped me the following season, but my batteries had long since been recharged. I was not prepared to take the easy option and let my playing career embark on a gradual slide towards oblivion. I felt I owed it to myself, as well as my club, to finish with a flourish.

Preece's injury presented my manager with the kind of emergency we had talked about in Germany. It left Skovdahl with little choice other than to recall me, for he required an experienced replacement. It would have been crazy, as well as grossly unfair, to pitch our young goalkeeper, Ryan Esson, into a struggling team. (By the way, you would be correct in assuming that, in addition to coaching him I take a fatherly interest in Ryan's progress. The age gap between us is 22 years.) I honestly thought I would be no more than a stop-gap until Preece was fit to resume, and was surprised when that did not happen. I think my boss was, too. It would be remiss of me not to acknowledge the encouragement I was given by both David and Ryan to keep my place. As I've said before in this book, goalkeepers tend to look after each other – even when they are rivals.

Ironically, David had been a sub for our fourth-round Scottish Cup replay with giant-killing Inverness Caley, but that was purely a precautionary measure. I had broken my nose and had 13 stitches inserted in my face after colliding with Aberdeen defender Derek Whyte in our 4–0 League win over Hibs at Pittodrie the previous Saturday. I was patched up for the replay but David, who had replaced me after 20 minutes of the Hibs game, was again on the bench in case my stitches burst. Come to think of it, my poor face has taken a fair bit of punishment in its time, but I've no complaints on that score. Goalkeepers expect to take knocks because it goes with the territory.

Any pain I've suffered has been more than compensated for by all the good moments I've enjoyed in the game. I know that for sure when I look at my collection of medals. It includes an MBE, and I know my family, who were at Buckingham Palace to see me being presented with it by the Queen, are especially proud of that award. I wore the kilt on that occasion, just as I had done as a member of

Scotland's squad at the World Cup finals in France five months earlier, and I can tell you that I felt quite humble. Especially when I heard what other recipients of awards had done to earn being honoured. Some had worked wonders for charity, others had risked life and limb in foreign parts, while all I had done was enjoy myself playing football. It gave me food for thought about how lucky I've been. I thoroughly enjoyed that visit to London because it was a family outing. In between being treated like royalty, Linda and the kids made sure my credit card took a pounding at the top department stores, but a shopping spree was no more than they deserved. They had suffered along with me during the bad spells in my career, when the thought of seeing a Manchester United reject meet the Queen prior to lunching at the House of Lords must have been beyond their wildest flights of fancy.

It is, as they say, a funny old game.

SIXTEEN

Looking Forward, Glancing Back

I'm proud of the fact that I was still a registered Aberdeen player, if only for another six months, when I celebrated my 42nd birthday last July. It was gratifying to be offered a new contract, even a short-term one, well beyond the age at which most of my contemporaries retired. Though manager Ebbe Skovdahl made it clear that he wanted me to concentrate on my new role as my club's full-time goalkeeping coach, I regarded his wish to have me on temporary standby as a compliment. An even bigger pat on the back from my boss was, of course, his public declaration that my most important task would be to produce a goalkeeper as good as myself. If I had not graduated from the school of hard knocks, that might have turned my head. Seriously, I appreciated what the manager said about me. It also helped soften the blow that came from knowing that I would not play again for Aberdeen other than in an emergency.

I never wanted to become known as the grand old man of Scottish football. That title seemed to creep up on me when I wasn't looking. You don't notice the years flashing past when you are enjoying yourself. Nor do I feel any different in terms of my fitness level or ability to do myself justice between the posts. If I did, I would never have agreed to carry on as a player – even in a standby category. I would not have risked embarrassing myself. On that score, it's not so very long ago that I was Scotland's first-choice goalkeeper, and I think it's worth remembering that the decision to quit the international scene was mine. Nobody pushed me out. It's natural, I suppose, that people who follow football take a keen interest in players who manage to extend their careers beyond the normal span. I'm always being asked if there is something special I've done in order to stretch mine over two decades. There isn't a straightforward answer to that question because, in the first place, you need luck.

And I can't claim any credit for the good fortune that enabled me to avoid career-threatening injuries.

While I've broken a few bones, I've never known what it is like to be sidelined by something serious enough to put a question mark over my future. What I do know, for sure, is that you won't get to the top – and stay there – without a lot of hard work. It's important that you set yourself standards in training as well as playing. Age should not be allowed to come into that equation, for once you use it as an excuse to ease off, you will find yourself on the slippery slope. A balanced diet has also kept me in good shape. I eat well but steer clear of junk food. Any drinking I do is restricted to social occasions such as weddings and nights out. It's never too early to start learning good habits, and I know my strict upbringing was a help in that respect.

When I first left home to join Aberdeen, I promised my parents I would not let them or myself down and that if I failed to make the grade it would only be because I was not good enough. I'm not trying to sound saintly, far from it, but I think that promise helped me find better ways to spend my spare time than joining some other young players in pubs or betting shops. I got myself an afternoon job at a sports shop and, during the summer, cleaned cars at a local showroom. I don't know if washing and polishing those cars helped build up my arm muscles, but it certainly felt like it!

Linda and I became engaged after my first year in Aberdeen, but there is no doubt that football played havoc with our courtship. During the time I was farmed out to Deveronvale, I was given only one weekend off in six to travel home to Renfrewshire.

It's a strange, almost unreal feeling when you come to the end of your playing career, especially one as long as mine, because you know your life has changed forever. You need to adjust to the fact that, even if you become a manager or, in my case, a goalkeeping coach, the best part of your involvement in the game will still lie behind you. That said, I've welcomed my manager's challenge. Hopefully, I can put my experience to good use and help Aberdeen's young goalkeepers develop their skills. I'll try to do for them what Erik Sorensen did for me all those years ago, although I did not appreciate his efforts on my behalf at the time!

While my post at Pittodrie is a new one, the fact is that I've been coaching Aberdeen's goalkeepers since last season. The manager asked me to take on that job following the winter break. I was reluctant to accept because former Scotland goalkeeper Jim Stewart, the man I was to replace, is my best friend and I did not want to take work from him. Jim, who is based in Ayrshire, is a travelling coach. He previously spent two days of his week at Pittodrie. Skovdahl decided, however, that he wanted a goalkeeping coach on the spot – and I was selected. I felt guilty, but Skovdahl eased my conscience when he told me: 'If you don't do this job, it will be someone else.' Happily, this situation did not affect my friendship with Jim. He remained my staunch supporter throughout the rest of that season.

I don't have any regrets about my playing days because any bad times were more than outweighed by good ones. I'm also glad that I had a full-time job outside football before I gambled on making the grade with Aberdeen because I could have returned to being a civil servant if that gamble had failed. Many of the young players of today do not have that kind of safety net because they join clubs straight from school. That doesn't look such a good idea when they find themselves, as so many do, tossed on the soccer scrapheap. If they haven't taken the opportunity to train for other work, they have nothing to fall back on. By the same token, I think it did me a lot of good to serve an apprenticeship in Junior and Highland League football before I played for Aberdeen.

I've always enjoyed seeing goalkeepers I've worked with make a name for themselves, and Bryan Gunn is a good example. Bryan spent a long time at Pittodrie as my understudy, but he went on to have a fine career with Norwich City and earned six caps. He showed that time spent standing in someone else's shadow need not be wasted, and that is one of the pieces of advice I'll give to any goalkeeper who works under my supervision. I don't have any doubts about the value of specialist coaching. I wish I'd had some during my early days at Pittodrie, but a lot of things have changed since then. What hasn't changed, of course, is that when you cross that white line your coach doesn't come with you. You are on your own.

I've never believed in settling for second best, and you won't find any runners-up medals in my collection. In fact, I've earned four – three with Aberdeen and one with Hibs – but I've no idea where they are. I suspect that Linda has them hidden away in a drawer. She knows I have no use for second prizes because I once tried to lose one. It happened after Aberdeen lost to Rangers via a shoot-out from the penalty spot in the 1987–88 Skol League Cup final. I was so disappointed that I didn't want to look at my runners-up medal and deliberately left it behind me at Hampden. As luck would have it, someone picked it up and handed it to Linda. Otherwise I would have managed to rid myself of an unwanted souvenir – just like the one I refused to accept as a Manchester United player. You may think that is an unreasonable attitude, but I don't. My message to Aberdeen's goalkeepers is that if they are happy to accept second best in any shape or form, the chances are that they will never win anything.

Another thing a goalkeeper needs, more so than any outfield player, is a sense of humour. His proximity to the crowd means that he cannot avoid hearing the jokes made at his expense, and some of them can be pretty pointed. I should know, for my cowboy legs, missing teeth and contact lenses gave my detractors a seemingly endless supply of ammunition. I never let it bother me. In fact I enjoyed the banter and know I will miss it because it is a part of playing. If you can't share a laugh with the fans, even if it is at your expense, then you are in the wrong business. I've had a good relationship with the supporters of all but one of the clubs I've served. The exception was Manchester United. I don't know why, but some of their followers seemed to have it in for me from the start. Cartoonists also found me a suitable subject for their wit when United lost goals, and one of them went so far as to caricature me as a man with no arms. I don't mind admitting that kind of ridicule was hard to bear, but I think I've proved it did no permanent damage to my self-esteem. If it had, I would never have been able to resurrect my career and make an international comeback. Incidentally, I enjoyed one of the jokes made about my two-minute involvement in last season's Tennents Scottish Cup final. It was pointed out that, despite the brevity of my appearance at Hampden, I still managed to stay longer in action there than Mike Tyson's opponent. Now that was funny.

I've said I have no regrets, but that is not strictly true. It was a big disappointment when the injury I sustained at Hampden led to me making only a fleeting appearance in my testimonial match against Middlesbrough. I also wish I could turn back the clock and start all over again.

Football has a habit of conjuring up strange coincidences. It was, for example, in a friendly against Middlesbrough that I made my top team debut for Aberdeen at Pittodrie all those years ago. I played for the first 45 minutes of that game with the English club whose goalkeeper, Jim Stewart, was to become my best friend. Even stranger is that fact that injury forced me to make an even quicker departure from my first game at Hampden than I did from the last one. In the interests of accuracy, that first game was actually at Lesser Hampden. It is also true to say it was contrary to my mother's wishes when I played there for Eastercraigs in an Under-18 League game against the Queen's Park club's Victoria XI. As I was due to sit an 'O' Level exam the following day, she thought it was a bad idea. She was right, for at the very start of that game I dived at a striker's feet and fractured my right wrist. Just like last season, I finished up in the Victoria Infirmary. But I can tell you I was more concerned about having to tell my mother that I would not be able to sit that exam than I was about my injury.

SEVENTEEN

Tips for Young Goalkeepers

Y ou'll never make the grade as a goalkeeper unless you master the basic art of catching the ball properly. That may seem a statement of the obvious, but the point I'm making is that this is the keystone of the job. Try to make a 'W' with your thumbs and index fingers when you field the ball from your neck upwards. Let the other fingers splay out and make sure that there is a gap of around an inch between the tips of your thumbs. Form another 'W' when fielding a ball from the chest downwards, but this time using your pinkies and ring fingers. *See Figure 1, page 161.*

Apart from being beaten by the sheer speed of the ball, there are three reasons for a goalkeeper failing to make a catch:

1. His technique is wrong.
2. He has lost his concentration.
3. His wrists and arms are not strong enough.

Technique is something you can work on, but concentration will only come through experience and learning from your mistakes.

You can, however, help yourself to stay alert by pretending that you are kicking every ball – even when play is nowhere near you – and talking to your team-mates.

I would say that 50 per cent of my job as both a club and international goalkeeper was about talking to and organising the players in front of me. Even when a corner is being taken at the other end of the pitch, you have to make sure that none of your defenders switch off and, as a consequence, are caught out by a counter-attack. If you do your job properly in this respect, you will have fewer saves to make.

Diving is the most spectacular part of a goalkeeper's work, but remember that looking good as you fly through the air will not improve your chances of preventing the ball from entering your net. Technique, not showmanship, is again the all-important factor in making this kind of save. *See Figure 2, page 162.* If you angle your dive in front of your line, rather than throw yourself along it, you will give yourself a much better chance of stopping a shot. You will find you have a longer reach, simply because you will have put yourself closer to the ball. Diving behind the line is not on, and this is one of the lessons I hammer home to the young goalkeepers I coach. I've also shown them that the angled dive can improve their reach by up to four ballwidths.

Another diving fault displayed by some young goalies is that they tend to land flat rather than the correct way, which is on their side. It's also important that the ball is the first thing to hit the ground because it will cushion your landing. Always keep your hands on top of the ball when you land, otherwise the impact will make it bounce out of your grasp. At primary school level, I've seen kids lose goals simply because they were frightened of the ball. Instead of attacking it, they let it attack them. As a result, they were caught on the back foot. A goalkeeper's body weight should always be forward. If he drops the ball, his momentum will give him a better chance of retrieving it. The proper technique in dealing with cross balls is to jump off one foot. If you jump off both, you don't have a forward momentum and, as a result, will be easier to knock off balance. Chances are you will drop the ball and finish up on your backside.

Former Manchester United goalkeeper Peter Schmeichel proved himself a master in the art of dealing with crosses during his time at Old Trafford. As well as his superb fielding of the ball, what caught my eye was the speed with which he then distributed it to set up an immediate counter-attack. While they cannot hope to throw a ball as far as the giant Dane, aspiring goalkeepers would do themselves a favour by trying to think as quickly as Schmeichel.

It's a mistake to face the ball squarely if it is being delivered from the flank, particularly in a free-kick situation. *See Figure 3, page 162.* You should be standing at an angle, so that you can see a wider view of the situation – as well as the kicker – without turning your head. I learned that lesson the hard way from Andy Ritchie, a fox of a player, in a match against Morton. Andy paused before taking a free kick from a wide position to make some signals. I fell for it and did exactly what he wanted by turning my head to see what was going on elsewhere. Andy then hit the ball with no backlift and by the time I turned back it was already heading inside the near post.

Every goalkeeper wants to savour the thrill of saving a penalty, and I was no exception. Unfortunately, I did not have a great record in this department and my former captain, Willie Miller, enjoyed reminding me of this. His recurring jibe was that Aberdeen might just as well have stuck a training cone in goal. Anyway, this does not disqualify me from passing on some things to bear in mind when you are facing a spot kick. Watch a player's eyes when he puts the ball down to take a penalty against you because he will probably steal a glance at the corner of the goal that will be his target area. The kicker will also be as edgy as you are, perhaps even more so, so keep him waiting for as long as possible. Remember that the good penalty-takers will always watch your feet. That tells them which way you have decided to move, so stand up as long as possible. Eric Cantona, another Manchester United hero, was the best I've ever seen in terms of waiting for a goalkeeper to commit himself, or at least give the Frenchman a vital clue as to his intentions.

It also pays a goalkeeper to stay on his feet as long as possible when he finds himself facing a striker who is bearing down on him in a one-on-one situation. If you stand up and make yourself as big a target for the ball as possible, it will pay dividends. A striker loves it when a goalkeeper comes out to dive at his feet because it makes up his mind for him. He can then dribble round you or knock it over your body. It's a different matter, however, if he finds you standing up, because he will then be obliged to make the first move. You have also made the goal look smaller. Provided a goalkeeper is properly balanced in terms of moving his feet and arms in either direction, he can cover a large chunk of the target area, and you would be surprised how many times he can stop a point-blank shot in these circumstances. Speaking from personal experience, I would put it as high as eight out of ten.

Some of you may recall that in Scotland's World Cup qualifying tie against Sweden at Ibrox in 1996, I managed to block a shot that was smashed in from only six yards. I must admit that the change of rule regarding pass-backs took a bit of getting used to, but today's young goalkeepers have no such problem. They've grown up with it. I would caution them, however, against taking unnecessary risks when they have the ball at their feet. I see no sense in the last line of defence trying to be clever by dribbling past an opponent. I've never had any reservations about kicking the ball into the stand when I thought it was the safest option. I've yet to see a goal being scored from row Z.

What every goalkeeper has to accept is that, like any outfield player, he will make mistakes. The difference is, of course, that his errors will always be regarded as more crucial. You can't change that because it is a fact of football life. What you can do, however, is put a mistake to the back of your mind as quickly as possible. It's history, so don't dwell on it or you will soon find yourself with more to worry about. Even if you have lost a bad goal, always try to make your saves look easy. You can deflate the opposition by doing this. If they, and their support, see you straining to reach shots and headers, it will lift them.

Goalkeepers need quick feet in order to react to situations, but that doesn't mean you have to be a track star. (Just as well or my career would never have achieved lift-off!) There are also plenty of exercises that will help your feet move faster. Although I much prefer game-related exercises to weight training, there is obviously a great deal of repetitive work to be done no matter how varied a coach makes his schedule. It's only by the constant honing of a goalkeeper's skills that you can help him improve. As I keep telling my charges, it will always be the goalkeepers who make the fewest mistakes who rise to the top.

Figure 1

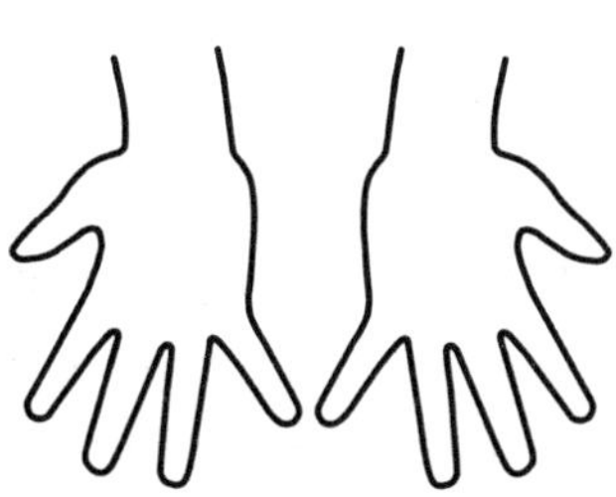

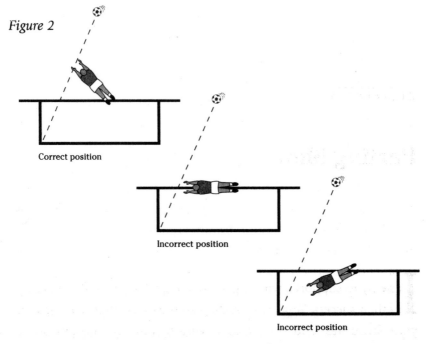

Figure 2

Correct position

Incorrect position

Incorrect position

Figure 3

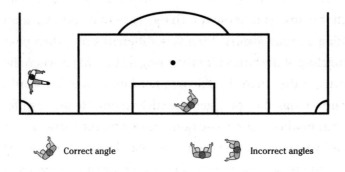

Correct angle   Incorrect angles

EIGHTEEN

Parting Shot

It's easy to support a winning team and bask in the reflected glory of their success. You enjoy reading all the praise that is heaped on your favourites, and you avoid having to put up with any snide remarks about them in the pub or your place of work. Life's a bowl of cherries, and there is a spring in your step every time you head for a match, because you know the chances are that you will soon be celebrating another victory. It's a very different story when your team is struggling at the bottom of their league, but that is when the real supporter, rather than the fair-weather fan, proves his worth. No matter how tough the going gets, he sticks it out. He won't suffer in silence, but neither will he lose faith and be marked absent.

All this is by way of saluting the remarkable loyalty displayed by Aberdeen's fans last season. Despite our team's abysmal showing in the SPL, they stuck with us through thick and thin – most of our 1999–2000 campaign being in the latter category. I thought that, because of my long career in football, I'd seen everything, but I was wrong. The backing our long-suffering fans gave us when we met Celtic in the CIS Insurance Cup final was out of this world. They turned out in force, turning their share of the ground into a sea of red and white, and proceeded to out-shout Celtic's following for most of the match. If you had wandered into Hampden after the final whistle, you would have found it hard to believe that Aberdeen had been beaten 2–0. Having stayed in their seats to the bitter end, our lot cheered us off the pitch and chanted manager Ebbe Skovdahl's name. I bet that was one of the few times in Hampden's history when the boss of a losing team has been treated like a hero. Aberdeen fans also did us proud in our Tennents Scottish Cup final against Rangers, although circumstances prevented me from enjoying their backing for more than a couple of minutes. I'm told they took our 4–0 defeat with commendable fortitude. My fervent hope is that such a remarkable show of loyalty will not go unrewarded, but time will tell. The certainty is that it would be unwise to assume that the patience of our support can be tried any further.

I wish I could say that Scottish football today is a better product than it was when I first started playing for Aberdeen, but I can't. It would be a barefaced lie and an insult to all the great professionals who crossed my path during the Pittodrie club's golden era.

Yes, our new, all-seated stadiums are fine, even if few of them hold big crowds on a regular basis, but there is not much else for us to boast about. What worries me is the lack of genuine quality where it matters most – on the pitches – and that situation seems unlikely to improve in the near future. I'm sure many Scots old enough to remember watching a far more attractive domestic game will share my view that our current dearth of home-grown talent has all the makings of a crisis. The warning lights are there for all to see. Top English clubs are no longer interested in maintaining even a fraction of their former level of recruitment from Scottish clubs, and our national team boss is operating under a tremendous handicap because of an increasingly restricted choice. It is obvious that Craig Brown's selection problems have been worsened by the influx of foreign players to our game, but that is not the only spin-off from this trend. I think it is also fair to say that the have-boots-will-travel brigade has failed to halt, or even disguise, a continuing downward spiral in standards.

Clearly, the financial clout of Rangers and Celtic has enabled them to hire, with the aid of massive transfer fees, a far better class of import than any of their SPL rivals. They are in a class of their own. The others, and that includes my own club, are obliged to rummage through the names of foreign players who are available through Bosman, the freedom of movement ruling which has changed the face of football in Europe beyond all recognition. They can get lucky, of course, and unearth a gem. But I have to say that, in some cases, our clubs are signing foreigners who are patently no better than the Scots they are replacing. They are also being paid higher wages. It's a vicious circle because bringing these soldiers of fortune into the Scottish game in such large numbers will make it even more difficult for a dwindling supply of talent on our own doorstep to come forward and claim first-team places. There lies the road to an uncertain future and, in some cases, perhaps even ruin.

Don't get me wrong, I'm not feeling miffed because it is far too late for someone like me to cash in on Bosman. Nor do I blame any foreign player, even a second-class one, for taking the chance to make more money in Scotland than he could earn in his own country. It's just that I care about our game's tomorrows, and they won't take care of themselves. We have to think very carefully about the direction in which we are heading. When clubs like Aberdeen and Hearts start talking about an urgent need to cut costs, it's cause for concern.

Another consequence of Scottish football becoming more cosmopolitan than I would ever have dreamed possible is that our clubs are losing their national identity. That saddens me, for I never tire of reminding young players that when Celtic, Rangers and Aberdeen won European trophies in Lisbon, Barcelona and Gothenburg, they did so with all-Scottish line-ups. When will we see their likes again? Never. Nor can we expect to see great Scots like Aberdeen's Willie Miller and Alex McLeish, Celtic's Billy McNeill, John Greig of Rangers and Dundee United's Maurice Malpas serving one club throughout their careers. Like this book, those days are over.

Statistics

Season 1982–83

1st Cap – Scotland 2 East Germany 0 (Glasgow) European
  Championship qualifier

2nd Cap – Switzerland 2 Scotland 0 (Berne) European
  Championship qualifier

3rd Cap – Belgium 3 Scotland 2 (Brussels) European
  Championship qualifier

4th Cap – Scotland 2 Switzerland 2 (Glasgow) European
  Championship qualifier

5th Cap – Wales 0 Scotland 2 (Cardiff) Home Championship

6th Cap – England 2 Scotland 0 (London) Home Championship

7th Cap – Canada 0 Scotland 3 (Edmonton) Friendly

8th Cap – Canada 0 Scotland 2 (Toronto) Friendly

Season 1983–84

9th Cap – Scotland 2 Uruguay 0 (Glasgow) Friendly

10th Cap – Scotland 1 Belgium 1 (Glasgow) European
   Championship qualifier
11th Cap – Northern Ireland 2 Scotland 0 (Belfast) Home
   Championship
12th Cap – Scotland 2 Wales 1 (Glasgow) Home Championship
13th Cap – Scotland 1 England 1 (Glasgow) Home Championship
14th Cap – France 2 Scotland 0 (Marseilles) Friendly

Season 1984–85

15th Cap – Scotland 6 Yugoslavia 1 (Glasgow) friendly
16th Cap – Scotland 3 Iceland 0 (Glasgow) World Cup qualifier
17th Cap – Scotland 3 Spain 1 (Glasgow) World Cup qualifier
18th Cap – Spain 1 Scotland 0 (Seville) World Cup qualifier
19th Cap – Scotland 0 Wales 1 (Glasgow) World Cup qualifier
20th Cap – Scotland 1 England 0 (Glasgow) Rous Cup
21st Cap – Iceland 0 Scotland 1 (Reykjavik) World Cup qualifier

Season 1985–86

22nd Cap – Wales 1 Scotland 1 (Cardiff) World Cup qualifier
   (replaced by Alan Rough at interval)
23rd Cap – Scotland 0 East Germany 0 (Glasgow) Friendly
   (replaced by Andy Goram in 47th minute)
24th Cap – Scotland 2 Australia 0 (Glasgow) World Cup play-off
25th Cap – Australia 0 Scotland 0 (Melbourne) World Cup play-
   off
26th Cap – Israel 0 Scotland 0 (Tel Aviv) Friendly
27th Cap – Scotland 0 Denmark 1 (World Cup finals, Mexico)
28th Cap – Scotland 1 West Germany 2 (Mexico, World Cup
   finals)
29th Cap – Scotland 0 Uruguay 0 (World Cup finals, Mexico)

Season 1986–87

30th Cap – Scotland 0 Bulgaria 0 (Glasgow) European Championship qualifier

31st Cap – Republic of Ireland 0 Scotland 0 (Dublin) European Championship qualifier

32nd Cap – Scotland 3 Luxembourg 0 (Glasgow) European Championship qualifier

33rd Cap – Scotland 0 Republic of Ireland 1 (Glasgow) European Championship qualifier

34th Cap – Belgium 4 Scotland 0 (Brussels) European Championship qualifier

35th Cap – Scotland 0 England 0 (Glasgow) Rous Cup

Season 1987–88

36th Cap – Scotland 2 Hungary 0 (Glasgow) Friendly

37th Cap – Scotland 2 Belgium 0 (Glasgow) European Championship qualifier

38th Cap – Bulgaria 0 Scotland 1 (Sofia) European Championship qualifier

39th Cap – Luxembourg 0 Scotland 0 (Esch-sur-Alzette) European Championship qualifier

40th Cap – Saudi Arabia 2 Scotland 2 (Riyadh) Friendly (replaced by Henry Smith at interval)

41st Cap – Malta 1 Scotland 1 (Ta'Qali Stadium) Friendly

42nd Cap – Spain 0 Scotland 0 (Madrid) Friendly (last game before being transferred from Aberdeen to Manchester United)

43rd Cap – Scotland 0 Colombia 0 (Glasgow) Friendly

44th Cap – England 1 Scotland 0 (London) Rous Cup

Season 1988–89

45th Cap – Norway 1 Scotland 2 (Oslo) World Cup qualifier

46th Cap – Cyprus 2 Scotland 3 (Limassol) World Cup qualifier

47th Cap – Scotland 2 France 0 (Glasgow) World Cup qualifier

48th Cap – Scotland 2 Cyprus 1 (Glasgow) World Cup qualifier

49th Cap – Scotland 0 England 2 (Glasgow) Rous Cup

50th Cap – Scotland 2 Chile 0 (Glasgow) Rous Cup (captain)

Season 1989–90

51st cap – Yugoslavia 3 Scotland 1 (Zagreb) World Cup qualifier

52nd Cap – France 3 Scotland 0 (Paris) World Cup qualifier

53rd Cap – Scotland 1 Norway 1 (Glasgow) World Cup qualifier

54th Cap – Scotland 1 Argentina 0 (Glasgow) Friendly (new cap record for Scotland goalkeeper)

55th Cap – Malta 1 Scotland 2 (Ta'Qali Stadium) Friendly (replaced Andy Goram at half-time)

56th Cap – Scotland 0 Costa Rica 1 (Italy, World Cup finals)

57th Cap – Scotland 2 Sweden 1 (Italy, World Cup finals)

58th Cap – Scotland 0 Brazil 1 (Italy, World Cup finals)

Season 1993–94

59th Cap – Malta 0 Scotland 2 (Ta'Qali Stadium) World Cup qualifier (first cap as Hibs player)

60th Cap – Austria 1 Scotland 2 (Vienna) Friendly

61st Cap – Holland 3 Scotland 1 (Utrecht) Friendly (replaced by Bryan Gunn at interval)

Season 1994–95

62nd Cap – Greece 1 Scotland 0 (Athens) European Championship qualifier (replaced Andy Goram in 78th minute)

63rd Cap – Russia 0 Scotland 0 (Moscow) European Championship qualifier

64th Cap – San Marino 0 Scotland 2 (Stadio Olympico di Serraville) European Championship qualifier

65th Cap – Japan 0 Scotland 0 (Hiroshima) Kirin Cup (captain)

66th Cap – Scotland 2 Ecuador 0 (Toyama) Kirin Cup (captain)

67th Cap – Faroe Islands 0 Scotland 2 (Toftir) European Championship qualifier (captain)

Season 1995–96

68th Cap – Scotland 1 Greece 0 (Glasgow) European Championship qualifier

69th Cap – Scotland 1 Finland 0 (Glasgow) European Championship qualifier

70th Cap – Sweden 2 Scotland 0 (Stockholm) Friendly (replaced by Andy Goram in 73rd minute)

71st Cap – Scotland 5 San Marino 0 (Glasgow) European Championship qualifier

72nd Cap – Scotland 1 Australia 0 (Glasgow) Friendly

73rd Cap – Denmark 2 Scotland 0 (Copenhagen) Friendly (replaced by Andy Goram at interval)

74th Cap – United States 2 Scotland 1 (New Britain) Friendly

Season 1996–97

75th Cap – Scotland 1 Sweden 0 (Glasgow) World Cup qualifier

76th Cap – Scotland 2 Estonia 0 (Kilmarnock) World Cup qualifier

77th Cap – Scotland 2 Austria 0 (Glasgow)

78th Cap – Sweden 2 Scotland 1 (Gothenburg) World Cup qualifier

79th Cap – Scotland 0 Wales 1 (Kilmarnock) Friendly (replaced Neil Sullivan in 80th minute)

80th Cap – Malta 2 Scotland 3 (Ta'Qali Stadium) Friendly

81st Cap – Belarus 0 Scotland 1 (Minsk) World Cup qualifier (last game as Hibs player before move back to Aberdeen)

82nd Cap – Scotland 4 Belarus 1 (Aberdeen) World Cup qualifier

83rd Cap – Scotland 2 Latvia 0 (Glasgow) European
   Championship qualifier

84th Cap – Scotland 0 Denmark 1 (Glasgow) Friendly (replaced
   by Andy Goram at interval)

85th Cap – Scotland 1 Finland 0 (Edinburgh) Friendly

86th Cap – United States 0 Scotland 0 (Washington) Friendly

87th Cap – Scotland 1 Brazil 2 (France, World Cup finals)

88th Cap – Scotland 1 Norway 1 (France, World Cup finals)

89th Cap – Scotland 0 Morocco 3 (France, World Cup finals)

Season 1998–99

90th Cap – Lithuania 0 Scotland 0 (Vilnius) European
   Championship qualifier

91st Cap – Scotland 3 Estonia 2 (Edinburgh) European
   Championship qualifier

DETAILS OF INTERNATIONAL APPEARANCES AGAINST ENGLAND

1 June 1983, Wembley (attendance 84,000)
England 2 Scotland 0
Scorers – Robson, Cowans

26 May 1984, Hampden (attendance 73,064)
Scotland 1 England 1
Scorers – McGhee (Scot.), Woodcock (Eng.)

25 May 1985, Hampden (attendance 66,489)
Scotland 1 England 0
Scorer – Gough

23 May 1987, Hampden (attendance 64,713)
Scotland 0 England 0

STATISTICS

21 May 1988, Wembley (attendance 70,480)
England 1 Scotland 0
Scorer – Beardsley

27 May 1989, Hampden (attendance 63,282)
Scotland 0 England 2
Scorers – Waddle, Bull

UNDER-21 INTERNATIONAL APPEARANCES

Season 1978–79
Scotland 3 United States 1 (replaced Billy Thomson at interval)

Season 1981–82
Italy 0 Scotland 1
Scotland 0 Italy 0 (aggregate 1–0)
European Under-21 Championship (over-age player)

ANALYSIS

Kept 45 clean sheets in 91 full or part games. International career spread over 16 years. Including Under-21 matches, was selected by five successive Scotland managers – Ally MacLeod, Jock Stein, Alex Ferguson, Andy Roxburgh and Craig Brown.

CLUB RECORD FOR ABERDEEN

Season	Friendlies	Competitive	Totals	Shut-outs
1976–77	1	–	1	–
1977–78	–	–	–	–
1978–79	2	17	19	4
1979–80	2	2	4	1
1980–81	7	51	58	18
1981–82	7	58	65	29

1982–83	3	59	62	31
1983–84	9	63	72	39
1984–85	9	43	52	23
1985–86	6 + 1 sub	40	46 + 1 sub	18
1986–87	6	48	54	24
1987–88	4	59	63	36
1997–98	4	37	41	10
1998–99	3	24	27	5
1999–2000	2 + 1 sub	36	38 + 1 sub	8
Totals	65 + 2 sub	537	602 + 2 sub	246

OTHER CLUB APPEARANCES

Season 1988–89 – Manchester United
League (38), English League Cup (3), FA Cup (7), Football League
Centenary Trophy (3) TOTAL – 51

Season 1989–90 – Manchester United
League (35), English League Cup (3), FA Cup (7) TOTAL – 45

Season 1990–91 – Manchester United
English League Cup (1) TOTAL – 1

Season 1991–92 – Reading (loan)
League (8), FA Cup (3) TOTAL – 11

Season 1991–92 – Dundee
League (13), Scottish Cup (2) TOTAL – 15

Season 1992–93 – Dundee
League (8), League Cup (2) TOTAL – 10

Season 1993–94 – Hibernian

League (44), League Cup (5), Scottish Cup (2) TOTAL – 51

Season 1994–95 – Hibernian

League (36), League Cup (3), Scottish Cup (5) TOTAL – 44

Season 1995–96 – Hibernian

League (36), League Cup (2), Scottish Cup (1) TOTAL – 39.

Season 1996–97 – Hibernian

League (35), League Cup, (3), Scottish Cup (4), League play-off (2)
   TOTAL – 44